RIP

⋏ THE ADDISON–WESLEY NETWORKING BASICS SERIES

Focused and Concise Hands-On Guides for Networking Professionals

The Addison-Wesley Networking Basics Series is a set of concise, hands-on guides to today's key computer networking technologies and protocols. Each volume in the series covers a focused topic, presenting the steps required to implement and work with specific technologies and tools in network programming, administration, and security. Providing practical, problem-solving information, these books are written by practicing professionals who have mastered complex network challenges.

0-201-37951-1

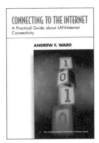

0-201-37956-2

0-201-61584-3

0-201-37924-4

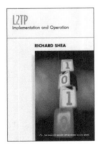

0-201-60448-5

0-201-37957-0

0-201-43320-6

Please visit our Web site at
http://www.awl.com/cseng/networkingbasics/
for more information on these titles.

THE ADDISON–WESLEY NETWORKING BASICS SERIES

RIP

An Intra-Domain
Routing Protocol

Gary Scott Malkin

Addison–Wesley

An imprint of Addison Wesley Longman, Inc.

Reading, Massachusetts • Harlow, England • Menlo Park, California
Berkeley, California • Don Mills, Ontario • Sydney • Bonn
Amsterdam • Tokyo • Mexico City

The publisher offers discounts on this book when ordered in quantity for special sales. For more information, please contact:

AWL Direct Sales
Addison Wesley Longman, Inc.
One Jacob Way
Reading, Massachusetts 01867
(781) 944-3700

Visit AW on the Web: www.awl.com/cseng/

Library of Congress Cataloging-in-Publication Data

Malkin, Gary Scott, 1961–
    RIP : an intra-domain routing protocol / Gary Scott Malkin.
        p. cm. —(Addison-Wesley networking basics series)
    Includes index.
    ISBN 0-201-43320-6
    1. Routers (Computer networks)—Standards. 2. Computer network protocols. I. Title. II. Series.
    TK5105.543 M35 2000
    004.6'2—dc21   99–049974

ISBN 0-201-43320-6
Text printed on recycled paper
1 2 3 4 5 6 7 8 9 10—CRS—0302010099
First printing, December 1999

This book is dedicated to Jon Postel, the first of the Internet's founding fathers to leave us. In my early years at the IETF, I learned a lot from Jon. I learned from the things he wrote, from the things he said, and from the things he didn't say. We all miss him.

Contents

List of Figures

List of Tables

Preface

There is no shortage of books that go into the gory details of routing. This is because routing is an art rather than a science. The concept is simple enough: Determine the best path between here and there. It sounds easy, doesn't it? Some of the protocols (RIP, for example) are actually pretty easy too. But the topologies on which routing protocols must operate are extremely varied and complex. All efforts to create a single routing protocol that can operate in all environments, on all topologies, on all systems, in an easy-to-manage manner, have proved unsuccessful. That is why there are so many routing protocols. In this book, we concentrate on one of the simplest, and one of the oldest, routing protocols: the Routing Information Protocol.

This book is divided into three parts. The first part describes several network topologies and discusses the pros and cons of the various routing protocols in each. This is important because a routing protocol cannot be described in a vacuum; it can be understood only in the context of the networks in which it is most suited to operate.

The second part describes how RIP operates in a network. It describes some common configuration parameters (including examples from several products), common problems that occur, and common solutions to those problems. Part II is addressed primarily to network administrators.

The third part covers the RIP protocol itself. It begins with RIP-2 [Malkin 1998], the newly deployed version, then discusses the enhancements over RIP-1 [Hedrick 1988]. It also covers some extensions to RIP, which are still in development or early deployment. Part III is targeted to protocol implementers.

Most of the material in Part III is taken from RFC 2453 (STD 56), the RIP-2 standards specification. That, in turn, contains RFC 1058, the original RIP de facto standard written by Chuck Hedrick [1988], and ported into RFC 2453 by Scott Bradner.

Throughout the book, key terms appear in **bold** the first time they are used; they are defined in the glossary at the end of the book. Some configuration parameters also appear in bold. The figures in the book use the following conventions:

Key to the Figures

This is a network node identified as node A. If it has a single interface, it should be considered a host; otherwise, it should be considered a router.

This is a network host.

This is a network router. It will have two or more interfaces.

This is an Ethernet segment. It may connect any number of network nodes.

This is a token ring. It may connect any number of network nodes.

This is a WAN link. It connects two distant routers.

This is a dial-up link. It connects a host to a dial-up server.

Acknowledgments

Much of the material in this book is taken from the RFCs for the Routing Information Protocols (RIPs). These protocols are a product of the RIP Working Group of the Internet Engineering Task Force (IETF). That's the source of the work, but the force behind the work is Mary Hart. Without her combination of patience and prodding I'd never have finished it.

Thanks also to the people who reviewed this book: Fred Baker, Darryl P. Black, Michelle Famiglietti, Joel M. Halpern, Mukesh Kacker, Gerry Meyer, Robert Minnear, John Moy, Matthew G. Naugle, John W. Stewart, III, and Dave Thaler.

Introduction

There are two major classes of routing protocols: **distance vector** and **link state**. The basic distinction between the two classes is quite simple, even if the implementations are complex. Distance-vector protocols operate by locally distributing global information. Link state protocols operate by globally distributing local information.

Consider the simplified topology shown in Figure 0.1. Using a distance-vector protocol, node C would advertise to nodes A and B that node D is one hop away and node E is two hops away. Node C would also advertise to node D that nodes A and B were one hop away. Node D would make similar advertisements with respect to node E. It should be clear then that each node is given reachability information from every other node (global information) by their neighbors (local distribution).

Using a link state protocol, each node would advertise to all other nodes (a process called **flooding**) the state of its links. Each node must then use a common algorithm to determine the topology of the network based on the link state advertisements. The Open Shortest Path First (OSPF) routing protocol [Moy 1998], for example, uses the Dijkstra algorithm [Sedgewick 1984] to make this determination.

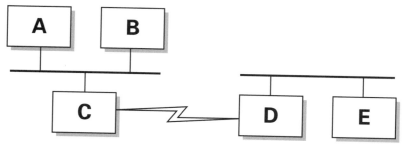

Figure 0.1. Simple network topology

Topologies and Protocols

1

Network Topologies

A network topology is simply a map that shows how the nodes on the network are connected by links. Nodes may be **hosts** (end nodes) or **routers** (intermediate nodes). Links may be **wide area networks (WANs)**, such as Frame Relay, ATM, and point-to-point; or **local area networks (LANs)**, such as Ethernet and token ring.

1.1 Simple Topologies

The simplest topology consists of two nodes connected by a point-to-point connection. A local area network (LAN) with several hosts but no routers is a trivial extension. In both cases, as Figure 1.1 shows, every node is directly attached (logically) to every other node. There is no need to do any routing.

The simplest topology in which routing is required is two LANs connected by a router. In this case, hosts on each LAN need to know whether the destination host is on the local LAN. If the destination is on another LAN, the host sends the packet to a router. In the case

Figure 1.1. No-router topologies

3

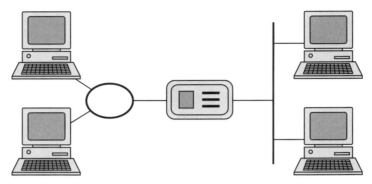

Figure 1.2. Single-router topology

of Figure 1.2, the hosts require only a default route to the single router on the network. Because there is only one router, IP requires no routing protocol.

Figure 1.2 also represents the simplest form of a **star topology**, wherein all of the **subnets** are connected to a central "hub" router.

One may reasonably ask why so few nodes might require a router at all. Why not simply put all of the nodes on a single subnet? The reasons, which depend on the application, include

- Address space—Some forms of LAN have limitations on the number of nodes that can be attached.
- Security—For administrative reasons, the nodes on one subnet might need to be isolated from the nodes on the other subnet.
- Traffic shaping—If many nodes are using one server, and many other nodes are using another server, it might be useful to split the two groups onto separate subnets to reduce collisions. Limiting the spread of broadcast traffic also falls under the heading of traffic shaping.

1.2 Structured Topologies

Once a network grows to a multirouter topology, there are basically two classes: single-path networks and multipath networks. Figure 1.3 shows a single-path, **tree-structured** network; Figure 1.4 shows a single-path, **hierarchical** network. Compare the two.

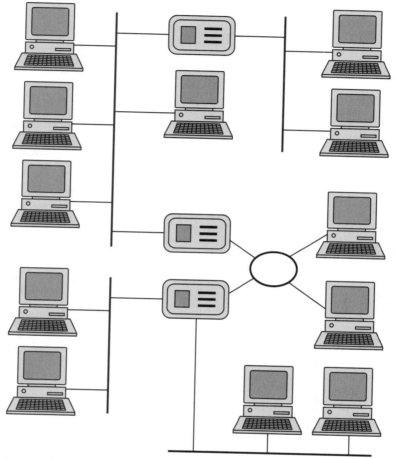

Figure 1.3. Single-path tree-structured network

The distinguishing characteristic of a tree, aside from its single-path topology, is that all of the subnets are peers. That is, there is no one subnet that interconnects the others. Note that the **diameter** of this network is three. That is, there are three hops between the most distant subnets. When a router is added to support a new subnet, the diameter of the network increases by one.

The hierarchical structure in Figure 1.4 clearly differs from the tree structure in Figure 1.3 in that the **stub** subnets communicate over a **backbone** network. The backbone network is typically a higher speed network than the stubs. In Figure 1.4, the Ethernets may be 10Mbps

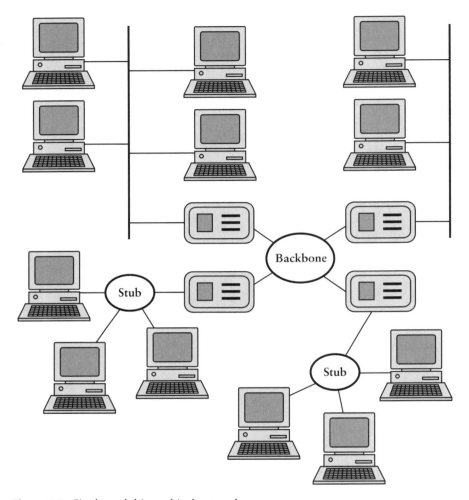

Figure 1.4. Single-path hierarchical network

and the small token rings may be 4Mbps, while the backbone ring may be a 100Mbps FDDI.

Note that the diameter of this network is two. However, should another router and stub network be added to the backbone, the diameter would remain two. Therefore, the advantage of a hierarchical network is the small, stable diameter of a larger network. The disadvantage is that the backbone represents a choke point and single point of failure.

1.3 Complex Topologies

Complex topologies include multipath networks and dial-in networks. Multipath networks offer multiple paths between at least two subnets. The paths may be of equal or different costs. In its simplest form, a multipath network uses two paths to provide redundancy, load sharing, or both.

Dial-in networks allow users to connect to the network via telephone lines (analog or digital) and establish their home host (e.g., a PC) as a node on the network. Note that this differs from dialing in to connect to a host as a terminal. The concept of dial-in host may even be expanded to include dial-in routers, which allow multiple hosts on a remote network to become part of the internal network.

1.3.1 Multipath Topologies

The topology in Figure 1.5 would most likely be a load-sharing scenario. For example, the nodes on network 1 would use router A to reach network 2, while the nodes on network 2 use router B to reach

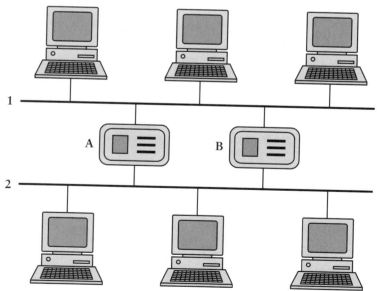

Figure 1.5. Load-sharing network

the nodes on network 1. Note that any connection between a node on network 1 and a node on network 2 would have asymmetric routes. That is, the path taken by a packet to go from one node to the other is different from the path a response packet would take. In this case, it makes no difference to either node. However, when the network includes WAN lines, it can make a difference.

The most common reason to create the type of topology shown in Figure 1.6 is to provide redundancy. One of the WAN connections would be a high-speed (e.g., T1) line and the other would be a dial-up 56Kbps line. If the primary T1 line were to fail, the backup 56Kbps line would be established. When the T1 was restored, the dial-up line would be dropped. However, there is no reason that both lines cannot be used

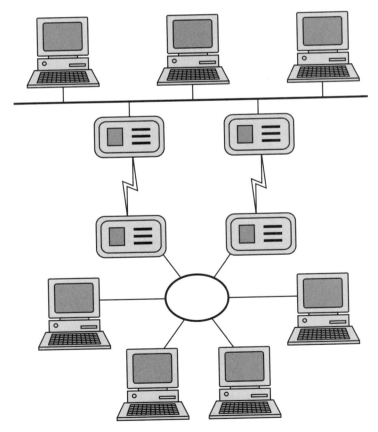

Figure 1.6. Redundant network

for load sharing. In fact, when redundancy is not a big issue, both lines could be load shared over a single pair of routers. The existence of two lines instead of one would be hidden to the hosts.

Because of the wide range of WAN line speeds, as opposed to LANs, asymmetric routing can produce some odd effects when the two lines are of greatly different speeds. This is discussed more in Part II.

1.3.2 Dial-in Topologies

The topologies described so far are essentially static. That is, unless there is a failure or a manual reconfiguration, the topology does not change over time. Such networks could have their routing manually configured by the network administrator using **static route** entries in the routers. With the introduction of a **remote access server** (RAS), part of the topology changes with every dial-in access.

Figure 1.7 shows the part of a network that includes a remote access server. If all of the dial-in lines are used by hosts (e.g., PCs), and all of the PCs share a subnet address, then this is, in fact, a simple topology. The router simply needs a **subnet route** for the dial-in hosts. However, if any of the dial-in lines are used by routers, then a routing protocol must be used to advertise the subnets on the far side of the dial-in router to the internal network. Whether the subnets in the internal network need to be advertised to the dial-in routers depends on the complexity of the dial-in network. In general, this advertising is not necessary because the dial-in network can use a single default route through the dial-in router.

A typical site has a network that includes some combination of the basic topologies shown. A corporate network, interconnecting multiple sites, includes most of the topologies and routing mechanisms described.

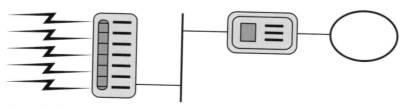

Figure 1.7. Dial-in network

2

The Basics

Before getting into the details of routing, let us review some of the basics.

2.1 The OSI Reference Model

Networking people often refer to the various layers of the protocol stack. These layers (shown in Figure 2.1) were defined by the International Standards Organization (ISO) in the Open Systems Interconnect (OSI) reference model. This model serves to distinguish the functions that occur at various points in the transmission and reception of packets in a network.

Layer 7 is the application layer. It is the interface between the user and the network. Some common Internet applications are electronic mail, World Wide Web, File Transfer Protocol, and TELNET. Technically, RIP is also an application, even though its "user" is IP.

OSI		TCP/IP
Application	7	E-mail, WWW, FTP, TELNET, RIP
Presentation	6	
Session	5	TCP, UDP
Transport	4	
Network	3	IP
Data Link	2	Ethernet, PPP
Physical	1	Copper, Fiber

Figure 2.1. OSI reference model and TCP/IP suite

Layer 6 is the presentation layer. It handles functions common to many applications (e.g., encryption, compression). In the TCP/IP suite of protocols, these functions are handled by the individual applications.

Layer 5 is the session layer. It manages the application sessions that are sharing lower-layer resources. In the TCP/IP suite of protocols, this function is handled by the transport protocols.

Layer 4 is the transport layer. It is responsible for end-to-end communication. In a connection-oriented protocol (e.g., TCP), it manages the connection. In a datagram-oriented protocol (e.g., UDP), it validates data and provides another level of multiplexing.

Layer 3 is the network layer. It is responsible for hop-to-hop communication. The Internet, for example, uses the Internet Protocol (IP) as its network layer protocol. While the network layer uses routing information to perform its function, the routing protocols are technically applications (layer 7).

Layer 2 is the data link layer. It is responsible for framing packets and managing the physical media. The most common protocols are Ethernet (on CSMA/CD* media), and the Point-to-Point Protocol (PPP) on dial-up/serial lines.

Layer 1 is the physical layer. This is the actual, physical media over which the bits travel (e.g., copper wire, coaxial cable, fiber-optic cable, radio).

The idea behind the creation of these layers was to have the ability to change the protocol in one layer without having to change the protocols in the layers above and below it. This goal has never been met. Applications depend on the transport services to ensure various levels of support, and the data link and physical layers are joined so intimately that frequently no distinction between the two is made.

---

*Carrier Sense Multiple Access with Collision Detection (CSMA/CD) is a media access algorithm. Multiple nodes on a shared media (MA) listen to the media for traffic before trying to transmit (CS). If two nodes transmit over each other (CD), they both back off for a random period of time and try again.

2.2 Names, Addresses, and Routes

There is frequent misuse of the terms *name, address,* and *route.* Radia Perlman created a very succinct way of distinguishing between these entities [1992].

X is a *name* if:
> X continues to work when node X moves, and X works for any node Y regardless of node Y's location.

X is an *address* if:
> X changes if node X moves, and X works for any node Y regardless of node Y's location.

X is a *route* if:
> X changes if node X moves, and X is different for nodes Y in different locations.

In other words, a name is portable, an address fixes a node's location, and a route describes the path between two nodes' locations. Consider the example shown in Figure 2.2.

"A" is a name because it works for all other nodes and it remains unchanged if node A moves from subnet 192.9.3.0 to subnet 192.9.4.0.

"192.9.3.1" is node A's address. It is an address because it works for all other nodes, but it would change if node A moves to subnet 192.9.4.0 (i.e., 192.9.4.1).

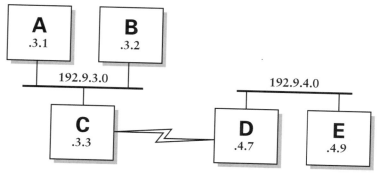

Figure 2.2. Names, addresses, and routes

"B→A" is a route from node B to node A. It is a route because
it would change if node A moved to subnet 192.9.4.0 (i.e.,
"B→C→D→A"), and it is valid only for node B (e.g., node C's
route is "C→A").

Node names are entirely arbitrary. That is, they have no inherent
meaning; they are simply labels that are convenient for humans to use.
Note that **domain names** do have structure, even if the component parts
are arbitrary.

Addresses, in IP at least, are not entirely arbitrary. While the network portion of an address is arbitrary (or assigned by the **Internet
Registry**), and the host portion of an address is arbitrary, the actual
address is a combination (according to a set of rules) of these two values
and, therefore, has a meaning.

Routes are determined entirely by the physical topology of the network and are not human-friendly. Policies can be created to force packets to take specific (usually suboptimal) routes, but no policy can force
a packet to take a path that does not exist.

While we are on the subject of nomenclature, here are a few more
confusing terms:

- **Network**   This is a heavily overused term. Its exact meaning
  depends on the context in which it is used. For example, when
  referring to layer 3 protocols (e.g., IP, IPX), a network is an
  addressable entity. With this definition, two Ethernet segments are
  considered one network if they are connected by a **bridge**, but two
  networks if connected by a router. Generically, "network" may
  simply refer to the topic at hand. Again, its definition is context
  sensitive.

- **Gateway**   This is the old name for a router. To be precise, a router
  is a layer 3 gateway, just as a bridge is a layer 2 gateway.

- **Interior Gateway Protocol** (IGP)   This is any protocol that passes
  routing information between routers within an administrative
  domain (i.e., a network, in the generic sense of the word). The
  name is a holdover from the days when routers were called gateways. RIP, IGRP, and OSPF are examples of IGPs.

- **Exterior Gateway Protocol** (EGP)   This is any protocol that passes routing information between administrative domains. It is also the name of an obsolete routing protocol. The most common EGP in use today is the Border Gateway Protocol (BGP-4). The term *gateway* was kept, instead of *router,* because the pronunciation of BRP would have been "burp."

- **Routing and forwarding**   Routing is the process of determining the best path to a destination. Forwarding is the process of accepting a packet on one interface and sending it on another. Therefore, the order of operations is receive, route, forward.

- **Units of data**   A unit of data is generally called a **packet** when it contains application data. However, *packet* has become the generic term for a unit of data. A **datagram** contains network-layer information, as well as the information passed down from the layers above. A unit of information moving across the physical media is a **frame**.

2.3 Subnets and Supernets

Generically, a network is a collection of nodes and the physical media that connect them. These media have associated addresses. These addresses can be subnet addresses, network addresses, or supernet addresses; however, the distinction can be subtle. Consider the topology in Figure 2.3.

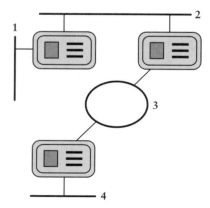

Figure 2.3. Subnets and supernets

It consists of four physical network segments (three Ethernet and one token ring). The best way to illustrate the differences in the nomenclature is by example.

- Assume that each physical segment is a logical subnet of the network 132.1.0.0/16.* Then, assuming a 24-bit **subnet mask**, segments 1 through 4 might have addresses of 132.1.5.0, 132.1.6.0, 132.1.7.0, and 132.1.8.0, respectively. Therefore, the topology represents a network composed of subnets.

- Assume that segments 1 through 4 have the following class C network addresses: 192.3.23.0, 192.3.34.0, 192.32.1.0, and 193.55.111.0, respectively. Then, each segment represents a logical network, and the topology is an internet (not to be confused with *the* Internet).

- Assume that segments 1 through 4 have the following 24-bit network addresses: 192.11.4.0, 192.11.5.0, 192.11.6.0, and 192.11.7.0, respectively. Then the topology is a supernet, represented as 192.11.4.0/22.

The examples show that a network is composed of subnets, a supernet is composed of networks with contiguous addresses, and an internet is a collection of networks.

The mask determines the type of address. A subnet mask has more 1-bits than the network mask. A supernet mask has fewer 1-bits than the network mask. When determining how to route a packet, a router will use the **longest match**. That is, a route with a host mask (which has 32 1-bits) is preferred over a subnet route, which is preferred over a network route, which is preferred over a supernet route, which is preferred over a default route (which has no 1-bits in its mask).

---

* This notation indicates an address of 132.1.0.0 with a 16-bit subnet mask of 255.255.0.0.

3

Static Routing

The simplest form of routing is static routing, as opposed to **dynamic adaptive routing**. The term *static* is taken literally to mean unchanging. A static route is created manually by a network administrator and remains in place until deleted manually by a network administrator. In some routers, if the topology changes due to a failure of a link or a router, the static route remains in place, even if it has been rendered invalid by the topology change. Consider the topology shown in Figure 3.1.

Assume router A is configured with a static route for subnet 3 via router B. If router B should fail (a **system failure**), router A would have an invalid route. In this case, the invalid route would be called a **black hole** because it points to an undetectable dead end. Packets sent by the host would be passed by router A to router B and lost because, having failed, router B cannot send ICMP [Postel 1981] unreachable messages back to the host. In another case, if the token ring should fail (a **link**

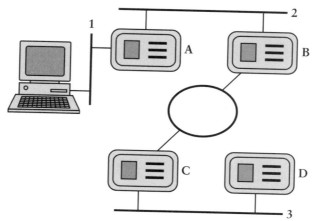

Figure 3.1. Points of failure

failure), the static route would still be invalid. However, it would not be a black hole because router B would have detected the failure and could send an ICMP unreachable message back to the host.

Even in networks that use a routing protocol, static routes are added sometimes to enforce routing policy, to point to the single exit from the network to an internet, or to eliminate the need to run a routing protocol over a dial-up link. This works because most routers give (or can be configured to give) static routes a higher precedence than learned (dynamic) routes (metrics of both routes being equal).

Suppose a network is connected to two **Internet service providers** (ISP). If one ISP has an **acceptable use policy** (AUP) that prohibits certain types of traffic, nodes within that network which generate that type of traffic must have their packets routed over the other ISP. This is an example of a routing policy.

Suppose you have users that dial into a network with dial-up routers (as opposed to simple nodes like PCs). The dial-in access device would generate a route to the dial-in router, but not to any network(s) on the other side of that router unless it received routing information via a routing protocol. The problem is that dial-up links are relatively slow (even a 56Kbps link is slow compared to a 10Mbps Ethernet). Sending routing-protocol traffic over that link is an inefficient use of the link's limited bandwidth, not that a routing protocol necessarily requires a lot of bandwidth. Instead, the dial-in access device can be configured to advertise the routes on the other side of the dial-in router whenever that router is dialed in.

4

Distance-Vector
Protocols

Distance-vector routing protocols have been used in packet-switched networks for almost 30 years. They were first used in the ARPANET, which evolved into the Internet, where they are still in use. In fact, two of the distance-vector routing protocols, Routing Information Protocol (RIP) and Interior Gateway Routing Protocol (IGRP) are deployed throughout the world.

Distance-vector routing algorithms are often referred to as Ford-Fulkerson or Bellman-Ford algorithms because they can be expressed in terms of the equations written by Bellman [1987] and Ford and Fulkerson [1962].

4.1 Distance-Vector Basics

Simply stated, a distance-vector algorithm operates by locally distributing global information. That is, each router knows the distance and next hop for every destination (subnet or host, if the distinction is being made) in the network. Each router then shares that information with each of its neighbors.

For the purposes of these protocols, a **neighbor** is any router that can be reached without passing through another router. For example, in Figure 4.1 routers A and B are neighbors; routers B and C are neighbors. But routers A and C are not neighbors. Routers connected by WANs are neighbors. All routers on a LAN are neighbors of each other.

In Figure 4.1, router B is the **next hop** in the path from router A to router C. It also happens to be router C's next hop to router A; however, this symmetry is not a requirement in larger networks.

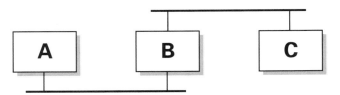

Figure 4.1. Neighbors

Each physical segment of a network, or **link**, that separates two or more routers has an associated **cost**. These costs are relative to the cost of other links in the network. That is, a cost has no meaning in and of itself, even if that cost is based on a physical property of the link (e.g., line speed). In IP RIP, for example, every link generally has a cost of one (representing a hop count). The cost of a route between two nodes is the cumulative costs of all of the links that must be traversed by a packet travelling between those nodes along that route.

4.1.1 Basic Operation

As mentioned, distance-vector routing protocols operate by exchanging routing information between neighboring routers. This exchange takes place for one of three reasons. First, a router issues a request for routing information (because it just came up, for example) and other routers respond to the request by sending their routing tables directly to the querying router. Second, each router periodically advertises its entire routing table to its neighbors (a **periodic update**). Third, a topology change occurs (a link goes down, for example) and the router advertises all changed routes in its routing table to its neighbors (a **triggered update**).

When a router receives an advertisement, it updates its routing tables with the new information. If this information causes a change in the router's routing table, it should send a triggered update.

4.1.2 Convergence

It is clear that the basic operation of a distance-vector routing protocol requires information about topology changes to be propagated from one neighboring router to another until all of the routers in the **routing domain** are informed of the total network topology. Therefore, there is a time interval between the occurrence of a topology change and the time the farthest router from the change receives the update. This time interval is the **convergence time** of the protocol. The longer this time interval is, the more packets may be lost to temporary black holes and routing loops. Most routing protocols have mechanisms for shortening this time.

4.2 First Distance-Vector Protocols

In the beginning, there was the Palo Alto Research Center for Xerox (PARC) Universal Packet Gateway Information Protocol (PUP GIP) [Boggs et al. 1980]; and it was good. It was the routing protocol for the family of Xerox networking protocols [Xerox Corporation 1981]. It served as the basis for the first protocol named RIP, Xerox Networking Systems (XNS) RIP. XNS RIP, in turn, was the starting point for the creation of IP RIP (used in the TCP/IP protocol suite) and IPX RIP (used by Novell).

IP RIP (now called RIP-1) was the basis for Cisco's proprietary Interior Gateway Routing Protocol and the Internet Standard RIP-2.

4.2.1 XNS RIP

XNS RIP is the most basic implementation of a distance-vector algorithm. It contains only those features that are required to determine the path between two nodes that contains the fewest hops. XNS supports two types of router: information suppliers and information requestors. During start-up, each type of router broadcasts a request for routing information. Information suppliers respond directly to the requestor. Information suppliers also send gratuitous advertisements every 30 seconds.

When an information supplier is shut down gracefully, it broadcasts a gratuitous advertisement to indicate that all routes through it are invalid. In order to detect a crashed router (i.e., it did not expire its routes), each router ages the entries in its routing table. When route information is received, the timer for that route is reset. In XNS RIP, if a route's timer reaches 90 seconds, it is said to have expired. This allows two (maybe three, depending on the timing) updates to be lost (datagram service does not usually guarantee packet delivery) before a route is considered bad. When a route expires, it is marked as unreachable; that is, its metric is set to infinity (16 in XNS RIP). The expired route remains in the routing table for 60 seconds. This allows the expired route to be advertised twice before it is deleted from the routing table.

The **expiration time** and **garbage collection time** have been chosen to strike a balance between the rapid recognition of a failed router and the prevention of spurious failure indication, which can generate a lot of extra routing traffic. For example, if the expiration time is 30 minutes, then a dead router might go undetected for that long. If it is 30 seconds, then a single lost update might cause a flurry of spurious "route dead" messages.

XNS RIP is designed to support small networks. It is not suitable for medium to large networks because of the bandwidth consumed by the periodic updates, and because it has an inherent network diameter limit of 16. Because XNS RIP considers only hop count to determine the best path, a network composed of heterogeneous network segments of widely varying bandwidth can produce suboptimal routes. Consider the example in Figure 4.2.

If the LANs are 10Mbps Ethernet segments, and the point-to-point link is a T1 (1.544Mbps) then, clearly, the path with more hops (A→B→C→D) is preferable to the path with fewer hops (A→C→D); however, XNS RIP will favor the path with fewer hops.

4.2.2 IPX RIP

IPX RIP contains two important extensions to the XNS RIP: split horizon and delay metrics. **Split horizon** is a mechanism that decreases convergence time by restricting the routes included in periodic updates. In

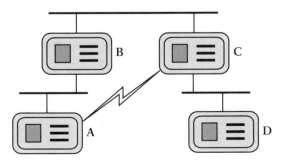

Figure 4.2. Route cost

the basic algorithm, all routes are advertised on all interfaces. The metric of each route has been incremented by the metric of the interface over which the route was learned (usually one). The result of this is that two routers, neither of which is the best next hop for a particular destination, will continue to re-advertise that route, incrementing the metric each time, until the metric reaches infinity, at which time it is deleted. This is called **counting to infinity** (see Section 8.2.2 Preventing Instability). Using split horizon, a route is not advertised on the interface over which it is learned. This eliminates counting to infinity between two routers, thus reducing bandwidth consumption and convergence time.

Delay metrics is a mechanism for including link speed in route calculation. In addition to carrying the hop count, each route also has an associated delay metric. The delay is kept in units called **ticks** (a tick is approximately 1/18 second). As a route is propagated through the network, each router increments the hop count and adds to the route's delay the delay associated with the interface over which it was received. Slower interfaces have larger delay metrics. Each router stores the cumulative hop count and delay for each route. The best route is the path with the lowest delay. If the delays are equal, the path with the lowest hop count is chosen.

4.2.3 IGRP

The Interior Gateway Routing Protocol is a Cisco proprietary distance-vector protocol. IGRP's extensions include a composite metric, type of service (TOS) route selection, load sharing across multiple routes, and holddowns.

The composite metric is a weighted combination of a route's capacity (channel occupancy in Cisco-speak), delay, and reliability. The formula is

$$\left(\frac{k_1}{C} + \frac{k_2}{D} \right) / R$$

C is the effective route capacity. It is the product of the route's bandwidth and the percentage of capacity based on the current load. The route's bandwidth is the bandwidth of the slowest link in the route. D is the route delay. It is a combination of the delays within the routers and the propagation delays of the links in the route. R is the reliability of the route. It is a percentage of the number of successful transmissions. k_1 and k_2 are weighting coefficients. They determine the relative importance of delay and bandwidth. By configuring these coefficients, a network administrator can select routes that provide a particular level of service.

IGRP maintains multiple routes to the same destination. If routes of similar cost exist to the same destination, IGRP will load-share across the routes. The definition of *similar* is the product of a configurable coefficient, k (variance), and the minimum route's cost. If k is set too large, undesirable routes may be included in the load-share set. In general, k is set to 1 (only routes of equal cost are to be considered for load sharing).

Holddowns help to eliminate large routing loops. Split horizon only eliminates loops between two routers. A router considers holding down a route if its cost is substantially larger than another route's cost to the same destination. The definition of *substantial* is a configurable coefficient usually set to 1.1.

4.3 RIP-1

For 20 years, RIP (version 1) was the distance-vector Interior Gateway Routing Protocol (IGP) in use in the ARPANET/Internet. It was based on XNS RIP.

RIP-1 uses a pure hop count for its metric; there is no consideration of link speed. However, network administrators can configure slow routes/links to increment the count by more than one. The drawback to this is the reduction in apparent network diameter (which is potentially severe because the maximum diameter is 16).

One improvement RIP-1 has over XNS RIP is an extension to split horizon called **poison reverse**. Where split horizon does not send learned routes out on the interface over which they were learned, poison reverse does send those routes. However, it sends them with a metric of infinity (16). Poison reverse reduces convergence time by immediately eliminating 2-hop routing loops instead of waiting for routes to time out.

4.4 RIP-2

In November 1998, RIP version 2 became an Internet standard. It has more or less displaced RIP-1, having been implemented by all major networking vendors. RIP-2 contains several enhancements to RIP-1, yet it remains forward compatible, thanks to the foresight of RIP-1's creators. The enhancements include the addition of subnet masks, alternate next hops, and route tags in routing entries; and the addition of security (authentication).

The addition of subnet masks in route entry updates allows RIP-2 to be used in environments with variable length subnet masks. In RIP-1, a router had to "assume" that the subnet mask for a route update was the same as the subnet mask of the interface over which the route was learned. That assumption became so critical to proper route determination that network administrators had to create their routing domains so as to ensure that the assumption remained correct. By including the subnet mask with each route, no assumptions need to be made. The route address essentially becomes a 64-bit entity (32 bits of address and 32 bits of subnet mask).

Route tags allow information from an EGP to be carried across a routing domain by the IGP. The use to which the EGP puts the information is transparent to RIP-2. RIP-2 is required merely to store the information, as it is received, in the routing table, then include the information in update messages.

Alternate next hops allow one router to indicate to other routers that it is not the best next hop. By default, the router from which a route is learned is the next hop. Alternate next hop is useful in environments that use multiple IGPs. Consider the example in Figure 4.3.

Suppose routers A and B use RIP-2, and routers B and C use OSPF. Router B can then tell router A that router C is the best path for routes it has learned from router C. The alternative is for router A to send packets to router B, which then forwards them to router C. This action is likely to generate ICMP redirect messages because router B is forwarding a packet out the same interface over which it received it.

The IETF requires security to be added to most protocols. It is especially important in routing protocols because of the roles they play in supporting the infrastructure of the network. RIP-2 specifies a simple,

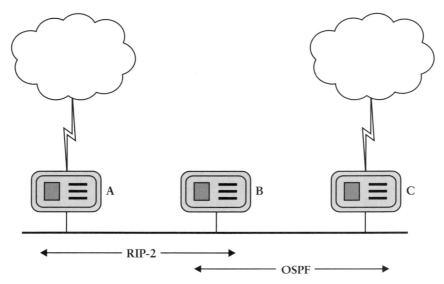

Figure 4.3. Multiple IGPs

clear-text password authentication mechanism. This is sufficient to prevent the injection of spurious routes into a network, provided the injector cannot capture valid updates and copy the authentication. However, the mechanism is extensible to include more secure authentication algorithms. In fact, such a mechanism is defined and is moving through the IETF standards process.

Additional extensions to RIP-2 are still under way, including modifications to support dial-up links efficiently. A version of RIP-2 for IPv6 [Deering and Hinden 1998], RIPng [Malkin and Minnear 1997], has also been developed.

Configuration and Operation

5

Configuration Parameters

In most topologies for which RIP-2 is the appropriate IGP, the default RIP parameters should be sufficient. In some devices, RIP is even active by default. Whether this is a good thing is a matter of some debate.

The basic RIP-2 parameters (i.e., those specified by the RIP-2 Management Information Base (MIB) specification [Malkin and Baker 1994]) include send and receive enable/disable, send and receive version numbers, authentication mechanism and key, and default metric. Many additional parameters are possible, including listing of valid routers, horizon control, and configuration of timeout intervals and retry limits.

5.1 Enable/Disable

RIP-2 may be enabled and disabled on individual interfaces. The MIB blends enable/disable with the version number controls (one for send and one for receive). In most implementations, the parameters are separate. This means that the MIB objects represent a combination of the settings of the enable/disable parameters and the version number parameters. When enabled, the MIB object returns the value of the version number parameter; when disabled, the version number parameter is ignored and "disabled" is returned.

It is not only legal, but perfectly reasonable, for the send and receive parameters to differ on the same interface. Consider the example in Figure 5.1.

If interface 1 connects to the main network, and the other interfaces connect to test networks, it is reasonable for the router to advertise the

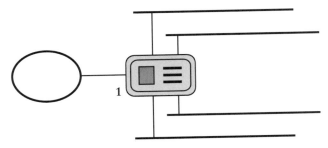

Figure 5.1. Unidirectional route advertisement

routes it learns from the main network to the test networks. However, it may not be reasonable for the router to listen to RIP advertisements on the test networks because they may use temporary, unassigned IP addresses; or, they may be running prototype routing code.

5.2 Version Control

There are two versions of **IPv4** RIP. Version 1 is now classified as historic. All sites are encouraged to migrate to version 2. In order to make the migration easier, version 2 routers support version 1 packets. However, although the packet formats are identical (version 2 packets merely use fields unused by version 1), version 1 routers cannot handle the extra information in version 2 packets. Fortunately, the creators of version 1 foresaw this problem and specified that a router (version 1) must ignore the information in the unused fields when the version number is greater than 1. This is a blessing and a curse. It is good that a version 1 router will not simply ignore version 2 packets; however, it becomes the responsibility of the network administrator to ensure that version 1 routers will not become confused by version 2 updates.

The primary reason RIP-2 was created was to allow RIP to operate in networks that use subnet masks of variable lengths. Remember that a router had to assume that the subnet mask of a route was the same as the mask of the interface over which the route was received. By allowing the specification of the subnet mask in each routing entry update, this assumption was no longer needed. The problem with a RIP-1 router hearing a RIP-2 packet is that the RIP-1 router still makes the assumption.

If that assumption is incorrect, routing loops and black holes may develop. The RIP-2 specification allows network administrators to control whether RIP-1 routers hear RIP-2 packets.

The version control parameters are per-interface parameters. That is, the send version and receive version may be configured independently on each interface.

The *send version* parameter has three settings (plus, potentially, "doNotSend"):

1. "1" indicates that version 1 packets should be sent to the **broadcast address**.
2. "2" indicates that version 2 packets should be sent to the RIP-2 **multicast address**.
3. "Compatibility" indicates that version 2 packets should be sent to the broadcast address.

It is important to note the distinction between broadcast and multicast. Version 1 and version 2 routers will receive a broadcast packet. This may lead to the problems of looping and black holes that were described earlier. Only version 2 routers will receive multicast packets (because the assignment of the multicast address post-dates the creation of the version 1 routers). Compatibility mode (as it has been called) has been deprecated with the widespread deployment of version 2 and should not be used unless great care is taken. Some routers do not even support it.

The *receive version* parameter also has three settings (plus, potentially, "doNotReceive"):

1. "1" indicates that only version 1 packets should be accepted.
2. "2" indicates that only version 2 packets should be accepted.
3. "Both" indicates that all versions (except version 0) should be accepted.

When a version 1 packet is received, the "must be zero" fields are checked for zero. If they are nonzero, the entry is ignored. In a version 2 packet, these fields are checked for validity. If the version number is greater than 2, the packet is processed as a version 2 packet except that the remaining "must be zero" field is ignored rather than checked for zero. A version 2 router that receives a version 1 packet must make the same subnet mask assumptions about the addresses as a version 1 router would make.

5.3 Authentication

RIP-2 has an extensible authentication mechanism. Described within the protocol is a simple, clear-text password. A specification for keyed MD-5 authentication has also been created [Baker and Atkinson 1997]. Two parameters are required to use authentication: *authentication type* and *authentication key*. The type parameter has three settings:

1. "None" indicates that no authentication is in use.
2. "Password" indicates that a clear-text password authentication mechanism is in use.
3. "Md-5" indicates that keyed MD-5 authentication is in use.

The key parameter specifies either the clear-text password or the MD-5 hash key, depending on the type setting.

It is important to note that only RIP-2 routers are able to authenticate. If a RIP-1 router receives an authenticated RIP-2 packet, the authentication will be treated as a bad route entry and ignored while the remaining entries are processed. In short, using authentication does *not* cause RIP-1 routers to ignore RIP-2 updates.

The clear-text password is only marginally useful. It will prevent an outsider from injecting false routes into a site's network, but it cannot protect against an intruder who can sniff the network (because the password is clear-text). It also prevents an out-of-the-box, unconfigured router from corrupting routing in the network.

The use of keyed MD-5 authentication can be very important to networks that are connected to the Internet, for example. Administrators typically think of attacks as being directed toward individual hosts (e.g., password cracking). However, since networking has become more the rule than the exception (we've moved away from large, mainframe clustering), hackers are now attacking the network itself. Consider this: If a hacker can easily capture sensitive data off the network, why go to the trouble of breaking into an individual system? One way to capture such data, if physical access to the network is difficult, is to inject spurious routing information into the target network to force packets to route through a host owned by the hacker. If the hacker then reinjects the packets, the victim is unaware that information has been stolen. Even worse, the hacker could alter the information prior to reinjection.

5.4 Default Route

In IP, the **default route**, specified as 0.0.0.0/0, is a special route. It specifies the next hop for any packet addressed to a destination not listed in the routing table. Consider Table 5.1, a condensed routing table (from a router whose address is 132.245.11.2):

Table 5.1. Condensed Routing Table

Destination/Mask	Next Hop
0.0.0.0/0	132.245.11.5
114.13.0.0/16	132.245.11.22
132.245.0.0/16	132.245.11.82
132.245.66.0/24	132.245.11.83

Assume that the site's network address is 132.245.0.0/16 and that the site's backbone network is 132.245.11.0/24. This table instructs the router to send all intrasite traffic to 132.245.11.82, except traffic to subnet 66, which goes to 132.245.11.83; and all extrasite traffic to 132.245.11.5, except traffic to network 114.13, which goes to 132.245.11.22. Without a default route, traffic addressed to an unlisted destination is simply discarded.

The default route metric parameter tells the router to advertise itself as a default router using the specified metric. Typically, only one router in a network is configured to generate a default route. The other routers propagate the default route throughout the remainder of the network, each adding to the metric. For networks with one access point to the outside world, the router that connects to that access point (i.e., the **border router**) is usually configured to be the default router.

5.5 Switches and Knobs

Engineers love switches and knobs. If there is more than one mode of operation for any facet of any protocol, there will be a parameter allowing the user to choose. Network administrators, and most people in general, are unable to pass up the opportunity to flip switches, push buttons, and turn knobs (it's the Curious Cat syndrome). When these two tendencies occur together, it creates a situation where configuration mismatches can render systems noninteroperable. Despite this well-known phenomenon, every RIP-2 implementation contains configuration options.

5.5.1 Access Lists

Access lists can be used to restrict transmission and reception of routing updates. A receive access list may be inclusive, to list the few routers from which updates will be accepted; or exclusive, to list the few routers from which updates will be rejected. A transmit access list is always inclusive because you cannot control to whom you do not send, only to whom you do.

By restricting the set of routers that share routing information, it is possible to establish multiple routing domains on the same physical network. It is also possible to create access lists that restrict the acceptance or advertisement of individual routes or groups of routes. This provides a finer level of control than restrictions based on routers.

5.5.2 Subnets and Supernets

The aggregation rule for RIP-1 was reasonably simple: Do not send anything that might be misinterpreted by the recipient. RIP-1 determined subnet masks using the following algorithm:

- If the address is equal to the address ANDed with its implicit network mask,* the address specifies a network route.
- If the address is equal to the address ANDed with the subnet mask of the interface over which the update was received, the address specifies a subnet route.
- Otherwise, the address specifies a host route.

---

* RIP-1 predates Classless InterDomain Routing and uses network masks associated with the three original classes (A, B, and C) of IP address.

For example, if a route update for 128.128.0.0 were received, it would be considered a network route because the non-network (host) portion of the address is zero. If an update for 128.128.64.0 were received on an interface whose subnet mask was 255.255.255.0, it would be considered a subnet route because the host portion of the address (i.e., the rightmost byte as specified by the mask) is zero. However, if the mask were actually 255.255.0.0, it would be considered (rightly or wrongly) a host route (with a host address of 64.0).

RIP-2 eliminates the guesswork by including the subnet mask with the route. However, that is only useful if all of the routers are RIP-2 routers. To prevent RIP-1 routers from receiving subnet routes that might be interpreted as host routes, a switch to control the sending of subnet routes should be implemented. A switch to control reception of subnet routes could also be implemented. Its purpose would be to limit the size of a router's routing table by accepting only network routes. This would almost certainly cause suboptimal routing (at best) and might create routing loops or black holes (at worst).

One feature of **Classless InterDomain Routing** (CIDR) is the creation of supernets. A supernet is to a network what a network is to a subnet. For example, the addresses 192.8.16.0 through 192.8.23.0 (eight networks with a subnet mask of 255.255.255.0) could be advertised as 192.8.16.0 with a supernet mask of 255.255.248.0. To make it more visible, consider Table 5.2, which shows these addresses in binary.

Table 5.2. IP Addresses in Binary

11000000	000010000	00010000	00000000
11000000	000010000	00010001	00000000
11000000	000010000	00010010	00000000
11000000	000010000	00010011	00000000
11000000	000010000	00010100	00000000
11000000	000010000	00010101	00000000
11000000	000010000	00010110	00000000
11000000	000010000	00010111	00000000

In binary, the supernet mask is

11111111 11111111 11111000 00000000

Clearly, this mask aggregates the set of networks into a single super-net. This aggregation makes more efficient use of the IP address space without increasing the number of routes being propagated through the network. The only requirement is that the addresses be aligned on the power-of-2 boundary associated with the number of addresses assigned. It should be obvious that RIP-1 could never support supernet addresses because of the subnet mask assumptions previously discussed.

5.5.3 Horizon Control

In RIP, *horizon* refers to advertised information limits. Specifically, when a route is learned over a particular interface, what, if anything, about that route is advertised over that interface? There are three modes of horizon control:

1. None, wherein a route will be advertised on the interface over which it was learned with its metric increased by the metric of the interface itself
2. Split horizon, wherein a route will not be advertised on the interface over which it was learned
3. Split horizon with poison reverse (or, more commonly, poison reverse), wherein a route will be advertised on the interface over which it was learned with a metric of infinity (16)

Running without some form of split horizon is rare because of the load generated by the need to "count to infinity" to determine that a route is invalid. Split horizon is sometimes used when the number of poisoned routes is very large and the topology is relatively stable; this reduces the load on the network and the routers without greatly increasing convergence time. Poison reverse is, by far, the most widely used mode of operation.

5.5.4 Timers and Timeouts

Most of the parameters discussed so far come under the general heading of "toggle switches," because they turn things on and off. The parame-ters associated with timer intervals and retry timeout counts come under the general heading of "knobs," because they vary the parameters' values. For RIP, several timer and retry values can be configured including update interval, time until a route expires, and time until an expired route is deleted. The latter two are typically expressed in terms of the update interval. Most implementations of RIP express these times as six update intervals and four update intervals, respectively. For example, RIP specifies that the update interval is 30 seconds, plus or minus a random factor to prevent routers from synchronizing. RIP also specifies an expiration interval (the time to wait after an update is received before considering the route invalid) of 180 seconds and a garbage collection interval (the time to wait after a route expires before deleting it) of 120 seconds. The intervals exist to ensure that a lost packet does not cause lost information; that is, things will retransmit to make up for a loss. Therefore, some implementations might have three independent time parameters, but most have a single time parameter and two retransmit-count parameters.

The default values were chosen to balance the need for rapid detection of a topology change against the desire to minimize spurious error indications. For example, if a router considered a single missed update to be an indication that another router had gone down, then it would send out an update invalidating the "down" router's routes. Then, 30 seconds later, it would receive an update and have to revalidate the same routes. Obviously, this involves a lot of unnecessary traffic (because all of the updates are propagated throughout the network) and routing table computation. On the other hand, if a router were to go down, the routes through it would become black holes until the other routers finally expire the routes.

The danger with changing timer values occurs when all of the routers in a network are not configured with the same values. Since a router expects updates with the same frequency that it sends them, a router with a short interval would be more likely to expire routes from a router with a long interval on only a single packet loss.

6

System Configuration

Having discussed configuration options in general, we will now focus on a few widely deployed systems and discuss their configuration options.

Most systems have local (e.g., TELNET, directly attached console) and remote (e.g., SNMP) configuration mechanisms. This section focuses on local administration.

Screen images taken from the various systems are displayed as follows:

```
What the system displays looks like this.
What the user enters looks like this.
```

6.1 Nortel Networks 5399/RA8000

The Nortel Networks (née Bay Networks) 5399 and RA8000 share a user interface.

There are three types of parameters: system-level generic parameters, which include parameters dealing with routing in general; system-level router parameters, which deal with routing and RIP; and per-interface routing parameters, which deal with RIP configuration for each interface.

6.1.1 System Generic Parameters

The following screen image (the spacing and formatting have been altered to fit the page, but the content and parameter order are the same) is taken from a 5399. Note that super-user access is required to run the **admin** program. The 5399 uses an asterisk to indicate that the parameter's value has been altered from the default.

```
annex# admin
admin: show annex
```

```
Annex Generic Parameters

inet_addr:*132.245.65.8           subnet_mask:*255.255.255.0
pref_load_addr:*132.245.65.32 pref_dump_addr:*132.245.65.32
load_broadcast:*N             broadcast_addr:*132.245.65.255
load_dump_gateway: 0.0.0.0        load_dump_sequence: net
image_name:*"gmalkin/mdbp"          motd_file:*"motd.65net"
config_file:*"config.65net""      authoritative_agent: Y
routed: Y                                 rtable_size: 1
route_pref: rip                   server_capability: none
disabled_modules: vci                  tftp_load_dir: ""
tftp_dump_name: ""                ipencap_type: ethernet
ip_forward_broadcast: N               tcp_keepalive: 120
option_key: ""                      seg_jumper_bay5k: 0
session_limit: 1152                       output_ttl: 64
arpt_kill_timer: 20                    fail_to_connect: 0
mmp_enabled: N                         disable_unarp: N
```

The parameters of interest are **routed,** which enables all dynamic routing; **rtable_size,** which sets the size of the routing table (in kiloroutes); and **route_pref,** which sets the RIP/OSPF route preference.

The **routed** parameter is the global switch that controls dynamic routing in the box. If set to "no," only static routes and ICMP redirects will be used to route packets. If set to "yes," RIP is enabled and ICMP redirects are ignored. For OSPF to run, it must be enabled separately; however, the **routed** parameter must also be enabled. To run OSPF without RIP, RIP must be disabled on each interface (see Section 6.1.3 Interface Routing Parameters).

The **rtable_size** parameter sets the maximum size of the routing table according to Table 6.1.

Table 6.1. Rtable_size Parameter Values	
Parameter Value	Number of Routes
1	1024
2	2048
4	4096
8	8192

The **route_pref** parameter sets the routing protocol preference to either RIP or OSPF. This is necessary because the metrics used by the protocols are not comparable. Routes learned via the selected protocol are always favored over routes learned via the other protocol.

6.1.2 System Router Parameters

This (modified) screen image shows the per-box router parameters.

```
annex# admin
admin: show annex router
Router Parameters

   rip_auth: "<unset>"              rip-routers: all
   rip_force_newrt: off
```

The **rip_auth** parameter sets the clear-text password used by RIP-2 authentication. When set, authentication is enabled automatically; when unset, authentication is disabled. The password itself is never displayed by admin.

The **rip_routers** parameter specifies a list of up to eight routers to which periodic and triggered routing updates should be sent (unicast), in lieu of broadcasting or multicasting updates. If set to "all," routing updates are broadcast/multicast. This parameter does not affect the responses to queries for specific routes, but it restricts an "all routes" request to listed routers. There is no parameter to restrict reception of routing updates.

The **rip_force_newrt** parameter modifies the routes' expiration heuristic. According to the RIP specification, a route via next hop A should not be replaced by a route via next hop B unless the metric through B is lower. If replacement occurred when the metrics were equal, the route would constantly flip-flop between the two next hops. However, most routers implement a heuristic that replaces a route with an equal cost route if the first route has aged more than halfway to expiration. This reduces the amount of time that a potential black hole exists, and does not cause excessive route changes. If this parameter is set to "on," then the first route will be replaced by an equal cost route if even one update (as opposed to three updates) is missed. This minimizes the amount of time that a black hole route exists (if the next hop router is truly down); however, it increases the chance for a spurious route change. Although this wouldn't be particularly harmful, it would increase network load. Note that this is a variation of the knob associated with retry count modification.

6.1.3 Interface Routing Parameters

This (modified) screen image shows the per-interface routing parameters. The Ethernet interface (en0) is used in this example. Note that OSPF parameters are not shown here.

```
annex# admin
admin: show interface=en0
Interface Routing Parameters

rip_send_version:*2            rip_recv_version: both
rip_horizon: poison            rip_default_route: off
rip_next_hop: needed            rip_sub_advertise: Y
rip_sub_accept: Y                 rip_advertise: all
rip_accept: all
```

The **rip_send_version** parameter specifies the RIP version that should be sent on this interface. This parameter has three settings:

1. "1" indicates that RIP-1 packets should be sent to the broadcast address.
2. "2" indicates that RIP-2 packets should be sent to the multicast address.
3. "Compatibility" indicates that RIP-2 packets should be sent to the broadcast address. *Note: Compatibility mode is deprecated by the standard and should not be used.*

The **rip_recv_version** parameter specifies the RIP version that should be accepted on this interface. This parameter has three settings:

1. "1" indicates that only RIP-1 packets should be accepted.
2. "2" indicates that only RIP-2 packets should be accepted.
3. "Both" indicates that all versions (except 0) should be accepted.

The **rip_horizon** parameter specifies the horizon algorithm to be used when advertising on this interface. This parameter has three settings:

1. "None" indicates that routes learned over this interface should be re-advertised on the interface with the metric increased by the interface's metric.
2. "Split" indicates that routes learned over this interface should not be re-advertised on the interface.
3. "Poison" indicates that routes learned over this interface should be re-advertised on the interface with a metric of infinity (16).

The **rip_default_route** parameter specifies the metric that should be used when generating a default route entry in a routing advertisement. The valid range is 1 through 15. If "off" is specified, then no default route will be generated. If a default route is learned or a static default route is configured, that route will be advertised, as would any other route. If this parameter is set *and* a default route exists in the routing table, only the generated default route entry will be advertised (*not* the default route in the table).

The **rip_next_hop** parameter specifies the use of the next hop field in RIP-2 advertisements. This parameter has three settings:

1. "Never" indicates that the next hop field should never be filled in.
2. "Always" indicates that the next hop field should always be filled in.
3. "Needed" indicates that the next hop field should be filled in only when needed.

The value inserted into the next hop field is the next hop specified in the routing table entry for that route. A next hop is considered needed when the Next Hop Router is on the same interface as the advertisement is being sent *and* the route has been learned by some means other than RIP (see Section 4.4 RIP-2). This parameter is ignored if **rip_send_version** is set to 1.

The **rip_sub_advertise** parameter specifies whether to include subnet routes in routing updates. When sending RIP-2 updates, this parameter should be enabled. If RIP-1 routers will be receiving these updates, careful consideration should be given to this parameter.

The **rip_sub_accept** parameter specifies whether to accept subnet routes from routing updates. When receiving RIP-2 updates, this parameter should be enabled. If RIP-1 updates will be received, careful consideration should be given to this parameter.

The **rip_advertise** parameter can be used to filter route advertisements on an interface. A list of up to eight network addresses can be specified. If an address is not an intrinsic network address (non-CIDR), it is so converted. As routing updates are constructed, if a route's address falls within one of the network addresses, it is a match. The list can be inclusive or exclusive. If the list is inclusive, only routes whose addresses match (or are subnets or hosts within) a listed network are included in the update. If the list is exclusive, only routes whose addresses do *not* match (or are not subnets or hosts within) a listed network are included in the update. If "all" is specified, no filtering is done and all routes (except local loopback and proxy ARP) are included. If "none" is specified, no updates are sent on this interface (also setting **rip_accept** to "none" effectively disables RIP on this interface).

The **rip_accept** parameter can be used to filter route reception on an interface. A list of up to eight network addresses can be specified. If an address is not an intrinsic network address (non-CIDR), it is so converted. As routing updates are parsed, if a route's address falls within one of the network addresses, it is a match. The list can be inclusive or exclusive. If the list is inclusive, only routes whose addresses match (or are subnets or hosts within) a listed network are accepted from the update. If the list is exclusive, only routes whose addresses do *not* match (or are not subnets or hosts within) a listed network are accepted from the update. If "all" is specified, no filtering is done and all valid routes are accepted. If "none" is specified, no updates are accepted on this interface (also setting **rip_advertise** to "none" effectively disables RIP on this interface).

6.2 Nortel Networks CVX 1800

The configuration for the CVX 1800 is a tree structure. The IP router and the interfaces are each represented by nodes on the tree. Additionally, virtual routers (vrouters) and virtual points-of-presence (VPOPs) have RIP configuration commands.

6.2.1 Router Commands

The following commands affect the operation of RIP on the router. This affects routing for packets received on the trunk interfaces (e.g., Ethernet), and packets not assigned to a virtual router (see Section 6.2.2).

```
CVX>config
Entering Configuration Mode
config> configure system/ip_router/ip_rip
```

At this level, the following commands may be executed:

```
system/ip_router/ip_rip>show
  Members currently configured at this level:
    proto_v1_enabled false
    proto_v2_enabled true
    triggered_updates_enabled true
    auth_type none
    auth_key none
```

The **proto_v1_enabled** command enables RIP-1 on the CVX. The **proto_v2_enabled** command enables RIP-2 on the CVX. Both commands can be set to "true" or "false." If both commands are set to "true," then the CVX runs in RIP-1 compatibility mode (which is no longer recommended by the RFC).

The **triggered_updates_enabled** command enables the transmitting of triggered updates when a change to the route table occurs. Disabling triggered updates saves network bandwidth on systems with a high dial-in user turnover. The downside is that the route to a new user may not be propagated to the network for 30 seconds. In general, this parameter should be set to "true."

The **auth_type** command sets the RIP-2 authentication mechanism to be used. It can be set to "md5," "none," or "text." (See Section 5.3 Authentication for details on authentication.) If RIP-2 is not enabled, this command is ignored.

The **auth_key** command sets the RIP-2 authentication password or MD-5 key, depending on the authentication mechanism in use. If RIP-2 is not enabled or the authentication type is "none," this command is ignored.

From the ip_router level, a trusted host may be configured. This is the single host with which RIP information will be exchanged.

```
system/ip_router >configure ip_rip_trusted
system/ip_router/ip_rip_trusted>set trusted_host <ip-
  address>
```

6.2.2 Virtual Router Commands

The vrouters allow a CVX to be partitioned into logically independent routing entities. The following commands affect RIP operation on the vrouters:

```
system/ip_router/ip_rip>show
  Members currently configured at this level:
    private_flag false
    rip_cost 1
```

The **private_flag** command enables the sharing of private routes with other routers. If set to "false," private routes are kept private (i.e., they are not included in RIP updates). If set to "true," private routes are included in RIP updates.

The **rip_cost** command specifies the cost of using the vrouter. Valid values range from 1 through 16, inclusive. The default is 1, which makes the cost a simple hop count. If set to 16 (RIP infinity), the vrouter becomes a packet sink.

6.2.3 Virtual POP Commands

A VPOP is another partitioning mechanism in a CVX. It allows configuration to be set up based on a selector that identifies the VPOP (e.g., called number, interface id). The following VPOP commands affect RIP operation:

```
session/vpop #/local_user_group #/ip_local_session>show
  Members currently configured at this level:
    rip_accept false
```

The **rip_accept** command enables/disables RIP for the local user group within the VPOP. The default is "false."

6.2.4 Interface Commands

A CVX interface may be any one of the following:

- `shelf #/slot #/SCC/BIC/Ethernet #/ip_interface/ip_circuit`
- `shelf #/slot #/SCC/BIC/loopback #/ip_interface/ip_circuit`
- `shelf #/slot #/SCC/BIC/HSSI #/FrInterface #/FrLogicalIF #/ip_interface/ip_circuit`

The following commands configure RIP for a specific ip_circuit (as specified above):

```
. . . ip_circuit>show
Members currently configured at this level:
   rip_v1_enabled false
   rip_v2_enabled false
   rip_send_enabled false
   rip_recv_enabled false
   rip_poison_reverse_enabled false
   rip_inflation_metric 0
   rip_cost 1
```

The **rip_v1_enabled** command enables RIP-1 on the interface. The **rip_v2_enabled** command enables RIP-2 on the interface. Both commands can be set to "true" or "false." If both commands are set to "true," then the interface runs in RIP-1 compatibility mode (which is no longer recommended by the RFC).

The **rip_send_enabled** command specifies whether to send RIP updates (including responses to queries) on the interface.

The **rip_recv_enabled** command specifies whether to accept RIP updates and queries on the interface.

The **rip_poison_reverse_enabled** command specifies whether to send poison reverse routes on an interface. If disabled, split horizon without poison reverse is done on the interface.

The **rip_inflation_metric** command specifies how much to add to a route's cost when advertised on the interface. This command can be used to bias the preference of routes to the same destination.

The **rip_cost** command specifies the cost (before inflation) of the route for this interface.

6.3 Cisco 3640

The Cisco configuration is managed through an interactive command system. Note that privileged commands must be enabled to configure the router.

```
cisco>enable
Password:<password>
cisco# configure
Configuring from terminal, memory, or network [terminal]?
   Terminal
Enter configuration commands, one per line. End with CNTL/Z.
cisco(config)#router rip
cisco(config-router)#
```

At this point, it is possible to alter the configuration of RIP in the system. The following commands alter the router's operational configuration.

The **auto-summary** command enables automatic summarization of network numbers. When enabled, multiple subnet routes for the same network, for example, will be aggregated and only the network route will be advertised. This results in reduced bandwidth utilization, coinciding with a reduction in the resolution of information being distributed. To disable summarization, use the **no auto-summary** command.

The **default-information originate** command configures the router to originate a default route. This route might be set in a border router through which traffic to the outside world should pass. The metric associated with the generated default route is configured with the **default-metric** command. To disable origination of a default route, use the **no default-information** command.

The **distribute-list** command allows routing information to be filtered based on the router from which it comes (**distribute-list gateway**), or on the prefix of the route (**distribute-list prefix**).

The **flash-update-threshold** command sets the time interval between a change to the routing table and the generation of a flash (triggered) update. It may be set from 0 through 30 seconds, inclusive. A lower value will decrease convergence time, but may generate more routing traffic. A higher value may leave the route to a new interface unadvertised, and therefore unreachable, until the next periodic update.

The **offset-list** command allows the metric of a route to be increased or decreased by a specified amount. This command can be used to set a preference for routes to the same destination.

The **output-delay** command sets the time interval between successive RIP update messages belonging to the same periodic update. It may be set from 8 milliseconds to 50 milliseconds. Increasing the delay is useful when a large routing table (i.e., a large number of updates each containing only 25 routes) must be sent over a WAN. A longer delay reduces the burst bandwidth consumption, which allows other traffic to get onto the wire.

The **passive-interface** command allows an interface to be marked as "receive only." That is, RIP updates are accepted, but none are sent. This command is useful when a remote site has several networks it wants to advertise into the central site, but does not need to know the list of networks in the central site (it may use a default route).

The **redistribute** command allows routes from other routing protocols to be "leaked" into the RIP routing domain.

The **timers basic** command sets the interval between routing updates. This should be changed with great care because multiple routers with different intervals can cause spurious triggered updates, routing loops, and black holes.

The **validate-update-source** command enables sanity checking of the source of the routing updates (e.g., Is the source directly attached?). To disable source validation, use the **no validate-update-source** command.

The **version** command sets the RIP version to "1" or "2." There is no support for RIP-1 compatibility mode (which is just as well).

7

Operation and Troubleshooting

In this section, we tie together the information presented thus far, and determine how to figure out what went wrong when something goes wrong.

All of the material in this section refers to the example network topology in Figure 7.1.

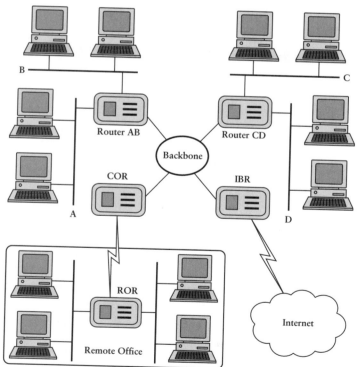

Figure 7.1. Example network 1

The router that connects subnets A and B is referred to as router AB. Router CD is similarly named. The central office router (COR) is connected by a dial-up link to the remote office router (ROR). The Internet border router (IBR) connects the network to the Internet.

The assumption is that there are many more hosts than shown. If there were only so few, it would make no sense to divide them so much.

7.1 Assigning Addresses

There are two common strategies of address assignment for this type of network topology. The first is to break a class B network into eight subnets (subnets A through D, the backbone, the dial-up link, and the two remote subnets). Using network 132.245.0.0 (remember, this is classful so a network mask of 255.255.0.0 is implied) and a subnet mask of 255.255.255.0, addresses might be assigned as shown in Table 7.1.

Table 7.1. Class B Address Assignment	
Subnet A	132.245.65.0
Subnet B	132.245.66.0
Subnet C	132.245.67.0
Subnet D	132.245.68.0
Backbone	132.245.1.0
Dial-up Link	132.245.30.0
Remote 1	132.245.31.0
Remote 2	132.245.32.0

The example addresses are arbitrary, except that ASCII 65 is an "A" and so on. It's cuter than just numbering one to eight.

After the routing algorithm has converged, and the remote office is not dialed in, the routing tables for the routers would appear as shown in Tables 7.2 through 7.5 (the entry for the backbone network is omitted because it never changes).

Table 7.2. Routing Table for Router AB

Destination Address	Next Hop	Metric
0.0.0.0	IBR	2
132.245.65.0	direct	1
132.245.66.0	direct	1
132.245.67.0	Router CD	2
132.245.68.0	Router CD	2

Table 7.3. Routing Table for Router CD

Destination Address	Next Hop	Metric
0.0.0.0	IBR	2
132.245.65.0	Router AB	2
132.245.66.0	Router AB	2
132.245.67.0	direct	1
132.245.68.0	direct	1

Table 7.4. Routing Table for COR

Destination Address	Next Hop	Metric
0.0.0.0	IBR	2
132.245.65.0	Router AB	2
132.245.66.0	Router AB	2
132.245.67.0	Router CD	2
132.245.68.0	Router CD	2

The routing tables show that no nodes are more than two hops apart, which is typical of a topology with a backbone network. They also show that packets destined to any network other than those in local topology are sent to the IBR, whose next hop is an Internet point-of-presence (IPOP) router.

Table 7.5. Routing Table for IBR

Destination Address	Next Hop	Metric
0.0.0.0	I-POP	1
132.245.65.0	Router AB	2
132.245.66.0	Router AB	2
132.245.67.0	Router CD	2
132.245.68.0	Router CD	2

When the remote office connects to the central office, the routing tables all change to incorporate the two subnets in the remote office. The new routing tables would contain the routes shown in Tables 7.6 through 7.10.

Table 7.6. Routing Table for Router AB

Destination Address	Next Hop	Metric
0.0.0.0	IBR	2
132.245.30.0	COR	2
132.245.31.0	COR	3
132.245.32.0	COR	3
132.245.65.0	direct	1
132.245.66.0	direct	1
132.245.67.0	Router CD	2
132.245.68.0	Router CD	2

Table 7.7. Routing Table for Router CD

Destination Address	Next Hop	Metric
0.0.0.0	IBR	2
132.245.30.0	COR	2
132.245.31.0	COR	3
132.245.32.0	COR	3
132.245.65.0	Router AB	2
132.245.66.0	Router AB	2
132.245.67.0	direct	1
132.245.68.0	direct	1

Table 7.8. Routing Table for COR

Destination Address	Next Hop	Metric
0.0.0.0	IBR	2
132.245.30.0	ROR	1
132.245.31.0	ROR	2
132.245.32.0	Router AB	2
132.245.65.0	Router AB	2
132.245.66.0	Router AB	2
132.245.67.0	Router CD	2
132.245.68.0	Router CD	2

Table 7.9. Routing Table for IBR

Destination Address	Next Hop	Metric
0.0.0.0	I-POP	1
132.245.30.0	COR	2
132.245.31.0	COR	3
132.245.32.0	COR	3
132.245.65.0	Router AB	2
132.245.66.0	Router AB	2
132.245.67.0	Router CD	2
132.245.68.0	Router CD	2

Table 7.10. Routing Table for ROR

Destination Address	Next Hop	Metric
0.0.0.0	COR	1
132.245.30.0	direct	1
132.245.31.0	direct	1
132.245.32.0	direct	1

The routing tables now show all of the routes associated with the central and remote sites. Note that the subnets in the remote site are three hops away from some others. This is because they are not directly attached to the backbone network. Note also that the remote office advertises its routes into the central office, but that the central office's routes are not advertised to the remote office. This is because the remote office only has a single path out, so a default route is sufficient. This mirrors the IBR's function of connecting the central office to the Internet.

The example thus far has used a subnetted class B network. However, IP address shortages being what they are, this type of assignment is rarely done for this size network. Today it is more common to create a supernet (using CIDR) out of eight consecutive class C network addresses.

Assume the site has been assigned addresses in the range of 192.0.8.0 through 192.0.15.0. Individually, each network has an intrinsic network mask of 255.255.255.0 (192.0.8.0/24, for example). Using CIDR, a single supernet is created: 192.0.8.0/21. By reducing the length of the mask by three bits, the eight individual networks are incorporated into a single supernet.

Consider the topology, with the remote office dialed in to the central office, when the class C networks are used to create a supernet. Assume the address assignments shown in Table 7.11.

Table 7.11. Supernet Address Assignment

Subnet A	192.0.12.0/24
Subnet B	192.0.13.0/24
Subnet C	192.0.14.0/24
Subnet D	192.0.15.0/24
Backbone	192.0.8.0/24
Dial-up Link	192.0.11.0/24
Remote 1	192.0.9.0/24
Remote 2	192.0.10.0/24

The routing tables for the five routers would contain the routes in Tables 7.12 through 7.16.

Table 7.12. Routing Table for Router AB

Destination Address/Mask	Next Hop	Metric
0.0.0.0/0	IBR	2
192.0.9.0/24	COR	2
192.0.10.0/24	COR	3
192.0.11.0/24	COR	3
192.0.12.0/24	direct	1
192.0.13.0/24	direct	1
192.0.14.0/24	Router CD	2
192.0.15.0/24	Router CD	2

Table 7.13. Routing Table for Router CD

Destination Address/Mask	Next Hop	Metric
0.0.0.0/0	IBR	2
192.0.9.0/24	COR	2
192.0.10.0/24	COR	3
192.0.11.0/24	COR	3
192.0.12.0/24	Router AB	2
192.0.13.0/24	Router AB	2
192.0.14.0/24	direct	1
192.0.15.0/24	direct	1

Table 7.14. Routing Table for COR

Destination Address/Mask	Next Hop	Metric
0.0.0.0/0	IBR	2
192.0.9.0/24	ROR	1
192.0.10.0/24	ROR	2
192.0.11.0/24	direct	2
192.0.12.0/24	Router AB	2
192.0.13.0/24	Router AB	2
192.0.14.0/24	Router CD	2
192.0.15.0/24	Router CD	2

At first glance, there does not appear to be much of a difference between the two address assignment strategies. Each allows for 254 nodes on each of the eight subnets; each has the same number of route entries in the routing tables. The difference comes from the fact that a class B address would have reserved an additional 246 subnets, using the same subnet mask, for a site that had no use for that many addresses. Clearly, this is very wasteful.

Given that the two strategies are the same internally, why not simply advertise the eight class C addresses? If this were the only site using

Table 7.15. Routing Table for IBR

Destination Address/Mask	Next Hop	Metric
0.0.0.0/0	I-POP	1
192.0.9.0/24	COR	2
192.0.10.0/24	COR	3
192.0.11.0/24	COR	3
192.0.12.0/24	Router AB	2
192.0.13.0/24	Router AB	2
192.0.14.0/24	Router CD	2
192.0.15.0/24	Router CD	2

Table 7.16. Routing Table for ROR

Destination Address/Mask	Next Hop	Metric
0.0.0.0/0	COR	1
192.0.9.0/24	direct	1
192.0.10.0/24	direct	1
192.0.11.0/24	direct	1

multiple class C networks instead of a single class B network, that is exactly what would be done. However, with thousands of sites using multiple network addresses, the routing tables of the Internet's backbone routers would quickly become flooded. This is what makes supernetting with CIDR so useful. Only a single route entry is necessary for other sites in the Internet to reach this site.

Even more compact use of the address space is possible. Notice that the dial-up link between the COR and the ROR uses only two IP addresses (one for each end point), but 254 are allocated. Suppose that the subnets in the remote office require only 20 or 30 hosts each. It would be possible to use a single class C address space and subnet it with a mask of 255.255.255.224 to create three subnets, each with a 30 host capacity. Using subnet masks of multiple lengths within one network is often referred to as **variable length subnetting**.

7.2 Getting Routers Talking

For such a simple network as this, RIP is the perfect choice for a routing protocol. With a class B address assignment strategy, RIP-1 is sufficient. When using supernet addresses, RIP-2 is required. The configuration for the routers is simple.

7.2.1 Configuration of Router AB

- Interfaces to subnets A and B—RIP should either generate a default route, or pass all routes. There will be nothing for the router to receive.

- Interface to backbone subnet—RIP should send and accept all routes.

7.2.2 Configuration of Router CD

- Interfaces to subnets C and D—RIP should either generate a default route, or pass all routes. There will be nothing for the router to receive.

- Interface to backbone subnet—RIP should send and accept all routes.

7.2.3 Configuration of the Central Office Router

- Uses a dial-up interface—no routes need to be sent. RIP should accept all routes. Some routers allow routes learned over a dial-up interface to be preserved and advertised over other interfaces when the dial-up interface becomes inactive. This allows hosts in the central office to activate the dial-up interface by sending a packet to a known destination. The problem is how to distinguish between a dial-up interface becoming inactive and going down (in which case the routes should be deleted).

- Interface to backbone subnet—RIP should send and accept all routes.

7.2.4 Configuration of the Internet Border Router

- Interface to the Internet. If RIP, rather than an EGP like BGP-4, is used, the router should advertise only the aggregate route for the network. In the classful example, this would be the class B address, 132.245.0.0. In the classless example, this would be the supernet address, 192.0.8.0/21. RIP should not accept any routes. A static route may be used instead.
- Interface to backbone—RIP should generate a default route; no other routes should be sent. RIP should accept all routes.

7.2.5 Configuration of the Remote Office Router

- Uses a dial-up interface—RIP should send all routes, but not a default route. No routes need to be received (or should have been sent).
- Interfaces to other subnets—RIP should either generate a default route, or pass all routes. There will be nothing for the router to receive.

7.3 Fixing Problems

In the network of Figure 7.1, there is not much to go wrong. A link may fail; a router may fail. In either case, there are no alternate paths—no way to automatically route around a failure. Consider the network in Figure 7.2.

Table 7.17. Routing Table for Router AB

Destination Address	Next Hop	Metric
0.0.0.0/0	IBR	2
A	direct	1
B	direct	1
C	direct	1
D	Router CD	2

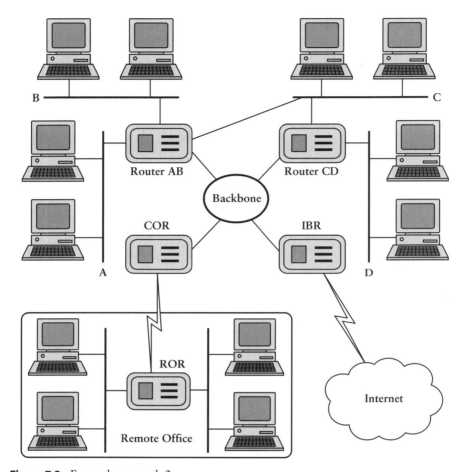

Figure 7.2. Example network 2

Note that a link from router AB to subnet C has been added. This link creates a cycle (loop) in the topology and alters router AB's routing table, as shown in Table 7.17.

Note that subnet C is now directly attached to router AB. Because the direct link has a lower metric than the path through router CD, given that all interfaces have a metric of one, the route advertised by router CD is ignored by router AB. Similarly, router CD ignores router AB's advertisement for subnet C because it also favors its direct link. The situation for the COR and IBR are more complex.

Because RIP updates from one router occur independently of updates from another, it is nondeterministic as to which router the COR and IBR will hear from first. It is entirely possible that the COR will use router AB as its next hop to subnet C, while the IBR will use router CD.

It is also possible that hosts on subnet C will experience **asymmetric routing**. For example, assume a host on subnet C is using router CD as its default router and the COR is using router AB as its next hop to subnet C. When that host communicates to a host in the remote office, packets destined to the remote office will use router CD and return packets will use router AB. In practice, this is not a problem, although it can make tracking problems difficult. For example, how can one debug a connection by tracing packets when the packets are taking different paths? The answer is to find the common points in the path and see where the packets are getting lost. In this topology, those points are subnet C, the backbone, and the dial-up link.

To debug a packet routing problem, it is necessary to follow the path of the packet *and* its response packet. There are tools to help to do this (e.g., **traceroute**), but they do not always give complete information, especially in the case of asymmetric routing. Given the path previously described, and assuming a failure of router AB, a **traceroute** from the subnet C host would show that the first hop was router CD, but no further information would be available. The **traceroute** would reach the COR, but the response would be lost. To find the problem, a line sniffer would be needed on the backbone. It would show the packet moving from router CD to the COR, and the response moving from the COR to router AB. Once the asymmetry is noticed, an examination of router AB would reveal the problem. Of course, this is a transient problem because the COR would eventually detect the failure of router AB and reroute traffic through router CD.

7.3.1 Routing Loops

A simple routing loop exists when two routers each consider the other the best next hop for a given destination. A complex loop involves more than two routers. When routing protocols are running properly, and no "human errors" have been introduced with static routes or routing policies, a routing loop should never exist after the routers converge. When a routing loop exists, even temporarily, the host originating the packet that becomes caught in the loop will eventually receive an indication (ICMP TTL exceeded) that the destination could not be reached. By running **traceroute**, it is possible to determine the nodes in the loop.

Without going into the details of how **traceroute** works, it displays to the user a list of the routers through which packets pass in order to reach specified destinations. If a router appears in the list twice, then a loop must exist. In the cast of a two-router loop, the addresses of the two routers will be displayed alternately.

7.3.2 Black Holes

Black holes are more difficult to find. The **traceroute** utility will show the routers up to the last router that responds. Then, that router must be examined to determine what is happening to the packets. The first step is to examine that router's routing table. Is there a route to that destination? Is there a route to the subnet or network for that destination? If neither, is there a default route? If the routing table seems to be in order, are there administrative filters (policy) on that router? Generally, when a packet is filtered, an indication is returned to the packet's originating host; however, that indication may be suppressed for security reasons.

If the router itself is not the problem, perhaps that router's outbound link has failed in a manner undetectable to the router (detectable failures would be handled by the routing protocols). If the link is operating correctly, perhaps the next hop router (at the other end of the link) has failed in some way. This type of failure would typically be detected by the routing protocols after some period of time.

Ultimately, it may be the destination host itself that has failed. In many cases, this is the best first place to look for a problem.

PART

III

RIP Specification

8

Basic Protocol

In a very large network, up to an international network like the Internet, it is highly improbable that a routing protocol will ever be developed that is capable of being used for the entire network. Far more likely, and the way the Internet operates today, is that the network will be organized as a hierarchy of autonomous systems (AS), each of which will be administered by a single entity (i.e., an administrative domain). Each AS uses the routing technology that most suits its needs.

Routing protocols used within an AS are referred to as Interior Gateway Protocols (IGP). Routing protocols used to connect autonomous systems are called Exterior Gateway Protocols (EGP). RIP is an example of an IGP that was designed to operate in moderate-size ASes.

8.1 Limitations of the Protocol

RIP-2 does not solve every routing problem. Despite decades of research and implementation, routing is still as much an art as it is a science. The following specific limitations exist:

- The maximum network diameter (i.e., the shortest distance between the farthest two points) is 15 hops, assuming that all interface costs are 1.

- The metric does not take delay, reliability, load, or transmission cost into consideration. Using a higher metric for a slower link can be done, for example, but that may affect the network diameter (which is already limited).

8.2 Distance-Vector Algorithm

As previously mentioned, distance-vector algorithms operate by locally distributing global information. That is, a router tells its neighbors about all of the routes in its table (with exceptions that will be discussed later).

If it is possible to get from node α (alpha being the beginning node) to node ω (omega being the ending node) directly (i.e., they are neighbors), then we may represent the metric (cost) of the hop as $\chi(\alpha,\omega)$. If α and ω are not neighbors, then the metric of a path between them, $X(\alpha,\omega)$, is the sum of the metrics of the hops on that path. The goal is to find the minimum cost path. To do this, we make the following statements:

- $X(\alpha,\alpha) = \infty$. The cost from a node to itself is infinite and therefore cannot be used in part of a minimum path calculation.

- $\chi(\alpha,\omega) = \infty$, when α and ω are not neighbors. If two nodes are not directly connected, the cost of the direct hop is infinite.

The minimum cost path's metric, therefore, is

$$X(\alpha,\omega) = \min[\chi(\alpha,\kappa) + X(\kappa,\omega)]$$

where κ represents an intermediate node.

If all interfaces have the same cost, then the minimum cost can be obtained by adding the interface's cost to the cost advertised by the neighboring node. Since all nodes operate in this way, the lowest cost path is always in the direction of the next hop that advertised the lowest cost. A node may keep all of the routes advertised by all of its neighbors, periodically looking for the lowest cost routes; or, it may simply keep the lowest route and compare all updates to that. In practice, most routers do the latter.

A proof is given in Bertsekas and Gallaher [1957] that this algorithm will converge in a finite time to the best values for $X(\alpha,\omega)$. No requirements have been placed on the order in which updates are sent or when the lowest cost route is determined. The only requirements are that nodes do periodically send updates and remember the lowest cost route, and that the network cannot delay messages indefinitely.

To summarize the operation of a generic distance-vector algorithm:

- Maintain a table with an entry for every destination. The entry contains the destination (address), the next hop (address) toward that destination, and the cost of reaching that destination.

- Periodically update every neighbor with each destination/metric tuple in the table. Note that the receiver of an update considers the sender of the update to be the next hop for all routes within that update (unless a RIP-2 next hop is specified).

- For each update entry received: If that destination is not in the table, add it; if the update is from the next hop, update the metric (higher or lower); otherwise, keep the route with the lowest metric.

8.2.1 Topology Changes

The algorithm described so far will find the lowest metric route between any two nodes given static conditions. In the real world, routers fail and links flap up and down. Extensions to the basic algorithm must be added to handle these cases. Consider the piece of a network shown in Figure 8.1.

Under steady state conditions: Node B would know that nodes A and C are neighbors; node A would know that node C is reachable via node B; and node C would know that node A is reachable via node B. If network 1 fails, nodes B and C will detect it, and node B would notify node A that node C is no longer reachable. However, if node B itself should fail, neither of the other nodes would be able to detect it. To handle this problem, distance-vector protocols must implement a mechanism for expiring routes.

In RIP, routers periodically (every 30 seconds) advertise their routing tables to their neighbors. Using Figure 8.1, the routes node A learns

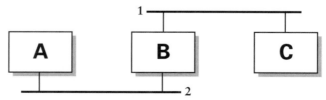

Figure 8.1. Network fragment

from node B are time stamped. Whenever node A receives an update for a route (even if no changes are made), it updates the time stamp. If too much time passes (180 seconds; 6 time intervals), the route is marked as invalid (its metric is set to infinity, which is 16). This invalid route is maintained in the routing table for some period of time (120 seconds; 4 time intervals) so that it may be included in advertisements to other nodes. The timeout periods are chosen to balance the need to detect failures rapidly and the desire to prevent spurious failure indications.

8.2.2 Preventing Instability

The current algorithm is sufficient to ensure that a node will be able to create a complete, correct routing table in a finite amount of time. To be useful, that time interval must be much less than the time between topology changes. If it is not, then loops and black holes will always exist somewhere because the routing tables will not converge. Consider the topology in Figure 8.2.

This network consists of four routers and six networks of interest. Four of the networks have a metric of 1, and one has a metric of 10 (the metric of the target network is of no interest). Each router will have a routing table containing a route to each network. For the purposes of this example, only the routes leading to the target network are shown.

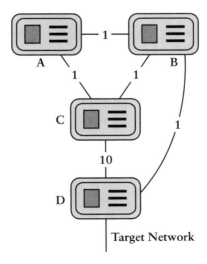

Figure 8.2. Loop topology

After the routing tables have converged, the routers have the entries (for the target net) in their routing tables (dc = directly connected; ur = unreachable) that are shown in Table 8.1.

Table 8.1. Routing Tables

Router	Next	Metric
D	dc	1
C	B	3
B	D	2
A	B	3

Now consider the case wherein the link from router B to router D fails. For simplicity, assume that all routers send updates at the same time.

Table 8.2. Routing Table Changes with Time

Router D		Router C		Router B		Router A	
Next	Metric	Next	Metric	Next	Metric	Next	Metric
dc	1	B	3	ur	∞	B	3
dc	1	A	4	C	4	C	4
dc	1	A	5	C	5	C	5
dc	1	A	6	C	6	C	6
dc	1	A	7	C	7	C	7
dc	1	A	8	C	8	C	8
dc	1	A	9	C	9	C	9
dc	1	A	10	C	10	C	10
dc	1	A	11	C	11	C	11
dc	1	C	11	C	12	C	12

Router B notices that one of its interfaces has failed and eliminates the route from its routing table. The problem is that the other routers have no way of knowing this, so, in the first iteration, they continue to advertise with unchanged metrics. Router B then picks either router A or router C (whichever update B receives first; it is nondeterministic, but unimportant) as its next hop. On the next iteration, when router B advertises its (incorrect) path through router C (in this example), router C then turns to router A as its next hop to the target network. At the same time, router A turns to router C. The routers keep advertising their mutually incorrect routes until the metrics become worse than the valid route through the costly link between router C and router D. The network then converges, as eventually it must.

The worst case occurs when a portion of a network becomes isolated (partitioned) from the rest of the network. In that case, the above pattern continues until the metrics finally reach infinity.

It should now be clear why it is desirable to choose a low value for infinity. It should be no larger than is necessary to handle the network's diameter. However, in order to guarantee convergence, all routers must use the same value for infinity. Therefore, all distance-vector protocols specify the value for infinity. For RIP, that value is 16.

There are extensions to the distance-vector algorithm to prevent "counting to infinity" problems. RIP uses split horizon with poison reverse and triggered updates.

8.2.3 Split Horizon

Metrics count to infinity when routers engage in a pattern of mutual deception, as router A and router C do in the preceding example. This pattern can be prevented by restricting the information advertised on a per-interface basis. Specifically, it is never useful to advertise a route on the interface over which it was learned. Not advertising these routes is called split horizon.

The problem with plain split horizon is that routers must use timeouts to eliminate routes that have become invalid. Split horizon with poison reverse does include routes in advertisements on interfaces over which they were learned, but it sets their metrics to infinity. By doing this, the fact that a route has become invalid is almost (see Section 8.2.4 Triggered Updates) immediately known to other routers.

Referring again to the network from Figure 8.2, if router A has a route entry to router D via router C, its updates to router C should indicate that router D is unreachable. If the route through router C is valid, then router C has a valid route to router D (either direct or via another router). However, router C's route cannot go back to router A because that forms a routing loop. Therefore, by telling router C that router D is unreachable, router A eliminates the possibility that router C might become confused and use router A as the next hop to router C.

Clearly, the advantage to using poison reverse is the reduction in convergence time. The disadvantage is the increase in the size of the routing updates.

8.2.4 Triggered Updates

If a topology change occurs early in the periodic update interval, it might take a considerable amount of real time before all of the routers are informed. Even worse, split horizon with poison reverse only prevents loops between two routers; a loop involving three or more routers still depends on counting to infinity for resolution. Having to count to 16 (by one every 30 seconds) would take eight minutes. Triggered updates can speed up the process significantly, thereby reducing convergence time.

To generate triggered updates, an extension is added to the distance-vector algorithm described thus far. When a route is added, changed, or expired, an update is sent almost immediately. The minimal delay, which varies by protocol, is included to allow multiple changes to occur prior to sending a triggered update (to reduce unnecessary overhead).

Several important points associated with sending triggered updates include:

- Triggered updates are sent independent of periodic updates and do not affect their timing.

- Triggered updates include only those routes that have been added, changed, or expired since the last update (triggered or periodic).

- Some mechanism must exist to limit the frequency of triggered updates to prevent network meltdowns.

9

Protocol Specification

RIP is intended to be a router-to-router protocol, notwithstanding the hosts that listen in order to find the routers on their networks. To be a router, a node must have multiple interfaces and be able to forward traffic between them. The networks associated with these interfaces are called **directly connected networks**. Each of these networks has three attributes of interest to RIP:

1. Metric (cost)—Since RIP uses a metric of 16 to represent infinity, valid metrics fall in the range of 1 through 15, inclusive. The most common value is 1.
2. Address—This is the IPv4 address of the network. It is valid to have multiple addresses per physical interface; RIP treats each independently. That is, it sends multiple updates (one per address) on the interface.
3. Subnet mask—This is the mask which, when ANDed to the address, yields the nonhost portion of the address.

Each router maintains a routing table. The routing table contains routes associated with the directly connected networks (often called interface routes), static routes (administratively configured), and learned routes. Each route entry in the table contains, at a minimum, the following information:

- Destination address—The IPv4 address of the destination. RIP-2 routers must also store the subnet mask associated with the address.

- Next hop address—The IPv4 address of the next router in the path to the destination. This field may be unused if the destination is on a directly connected network.

- Metric—The total cost of getting a datagram from this router to the destination. Typically, this represents the number of routers between this router and the destination (the hop count).

- Flags—At a minimum, a **route change flag** is required to support triggered updates. When set, it indicates that the route has been added, changed, or expired since the last update (triggered or periodic) was generated.

- Timer—There are several ways to implement the various timers (see Section 9.3 Timers) associated with RIP. At a minimum, the number of seconds since the last time the route was changed is required.

9.1 Message Format

RIP is a UDP-based protocol that operates on port 520. All updates are sent to the RIP port, from the RIP port. Queries are sent to the RIP port. Responses to queries are sent to the port from which the request came.

All fields in RIP messages contain binary integers (except as noted below) in network-byte order (**big-endian**). The RIP message format is shown in Figure 9.1.

Command is a 1-octet field that specifies the message type. The commands supported by RIP-2 are

- 1—request. This message is a request for all or part of the recipient's routing table.

- 2—response. This message contains a routing update. It may be the response to a request, or a periodic (unsolicited) update.

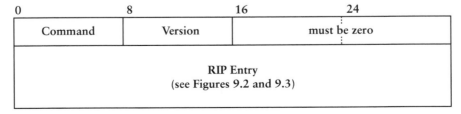

Figure 9.1. RIP message format

Version is a 1-octet field that specifies the version of the message. Only versions 1 and 2 are currently supported.

The "must be zero" field is two octets in length. It is reserved (by RIP-1 and RIP-2) for future use and must be zero.

The "RIP Entry" field is 20 octets in length. Its format is determined by the version of the message. If RIP-2 authentication is in use, this field has an additional format. There may be up to 25 RIP entries in a RIP message. This limitation ensures that the datagram will never be fragmented by IP.

A version 1 message has the RIP entry format shown in Figure 9.2.

Address family ID is a 2-octet field that contains the type of address being carried. RIP only supports IPv4 addresses (AF_INET – 2).

IPv4 address is a 4-octet field that contains the destination address of the route.

Metric is a 4-octet field that contains the metric of the route.

UNIX programmers may recognize that the first 16 octets are a sockaddr structure. This was done in case RIP was ever used for protocols other than IP. The metric is four octets merely to maintain alignment.

A version 2 message has the RIP entry format shown in Figure 9.3.

Address family ID is a 2-octet field that contains the type of address being carried. RIP only supports IPv4 addresses (AF_INET – 2).

Route tag is a 2-octet field that contains an attribute, opaque to RIP, that must be preserved and re-advertised with the route. It is intended to be used to differentiate between "internal" RIP routes and "external" RIP routes, which may have been imported from an EGP or another IGP running in the same routing domain. Other uses for this

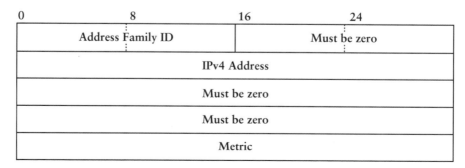

Figure 9.2. RIP-1 entry format

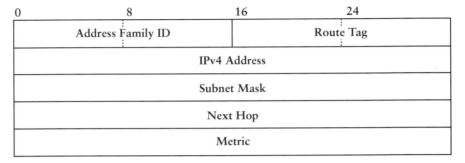

Figure 9.3. RIP-2 entry format

field are valid, providing that all of the routers in the RIP domain use it consistently.

IPv4 address is a 4-octet field that contains the destination address of the route.

Subnet mask is a 4-octet field that contains the subnet mask, which, when applied to the address, yields the nonhost portion of the address. Note that "subnet" is a historical name; the mask may, in fact, be a supernet, network, subnet, or host mask.

Next hop is a 4-octet field that contains the IPv4 address of the next router in the path to the destination. If this field is empty (0.0.0.0), then the next hop for this route is the router that originated the update. A router may also choose to ignore a specified next hop in favor of using the update's originator, which will produce a valid, if suboptimal, route.

Metric is a 4-octet field that specifies the metric of the route.

9.2 Addressing Considerations

Distance-vector routing can be used to describe routes to supernets, networks, subnets, and hosts. RIP, as a protocol, does not formally distinguish between these types of routes. To RIP-1, the address is an opaque, 32-bit entity. To RIP-2, the address and subnet mask form a 64-bit entity. However, table maintenance and IP forwarding certainly make such distinctions, which is why RIP-2 was created to carry subnet masks.

Nodes that use RIP information should use the most specific information available when routing datagrams. In IP, "most specific" means the address whose mask has the most 1's in it. Therefore, routes are generally preferred in the following order:

- host (whose subnet mask is always 255.255.255.255)
- subnet
- network
- supernet
- default

In IP, the default route is the route to use for all traffic for which there is no other route. It is specified with a special IP address, 0.0.0.0. The subnet mask for the default route is also defined to be 0.0.0.0. In standard notation, this would be 0.0.0.0/0.

RIP-2 carries a subnet mask for each destination address so there is never any ambiguity about the route's type. RIP-1 (the evolution of which predates subnets and supernets) does not carry a subnet mask and, therefore, must make assumptions about the route's type. It does this by using an address's **intrinsic network mask**.

IP (pre-CIDR) has three classes of routable addresses (multicast and experimental addresses are not routable in the usual sense). These classes are shown in Table 9.1.

Table 9.1. IP Address Classes

Class	Msb	Addresses	Hosts/Net
A	0	1.0.0.0–127.0.0.0	16,777,214
B	10	128.0.0.0–191.255.0.0	65,534
C	110	192.0.0.0–223.255.255.0	254

An address's class is determined by its most significant bits (leftmost bits in the leftmost octet). As shown in Table 9.1, class A addresses have one octet of network address and three octets of host address, making the intrinsic network mask 255.0.0.0. Class B addresses have two octets of network address and two octets of host address, making the mask 255.255.0.0. Class C addresses have three octets of network address and one octet of host address, making the mask 255.255.255.0. Clearly, class A addresses are very large, but there are very few, while class C addresses are very small, but there are a lot of them.

RIP-1's rules for determining the address type are as follows:

- If the destination address ANDed with its intrinsic network mask is equal to the destination address, the route is a network route.
- If the destination address ANDed with the subnet mask of the interface over which the route was learned is equal to the destination address, the route is a subnet route.
- Otherwise, the route is a host route.

The test for subnet route is a heuristic, but most implementations support it. Note that supernet routes are not supported in RIP-1.

The most important addressing consideration is the dissemination of the information. When RIP-1 is in use, RIP-2 routers must not leak information that does not meet RIP-1's rules onto a subnet on which a RIP-1 router resides. Border routers should not leak subnet information outside the routing domain, but should send only network routes (anything else would defeat the purpose of a routing hierarchy). Dissemination of the default route must also be controlled carefully. However, the mechanisms for restricting information are not a formal part of the protocol, and are left to the implementers and network administrators.

9.3 Timers

There are several time-based events in RIP: periodic updates, triggered update delays, and route expiration and deletion periods. The default values specified for these events are part of the RIP standard. Some implementations allow these values to be configured, but they should be changed only with extreme caution. Consider the case of a router configured with a 5-second interval, while the other routers use the default of 30 seconds. Because this router sends updates every 5 seconds, it expects to hear updates every 5 seconds. The 30-second interval puts the other routers' updates on the edge of being deleted; a single lost update would guarantee it.

9.3.1 Periodic Updates

Every 30 seconds, a RIP router sends an unsolicited response message (update) to all of its neighbors on all of its interfaces. These updates contain the entire routing table, subject to split horizon (see Section 8.2.3 Split Horizon) and administration restriction (filtering).

When several nodes are connected on broadcast media, there is a tendency for them to synchronize such that they all send their updates at the same time. This is undesirable because of the network load spike, which interferes with other traffic, and the number of collisions, which could lead to spurious route timeouts. To prevent these problems, router implementations must provide one of the following mechanisms:

- The timer must be triggered by a clock that is not affected by system or network load, or by the time required to service other timer events.

- Each timer interval must be offset by a random time (± 5 seconds). Research indicates that larger offsets may be more beneficial [Floyd and Jacobson 1993].

9.3.2 Triggered Update Delays

In order to limit the number of triggered updates generated by frequent topology changes (which might be caused by dial-in traffic, for example), the updates should be delayed by a small random amount of time (up to 5 seconds, for example). When the update is sent, only routes that have changed since the last update (triggered or periodic) should be included, subject to split horizon and administrative restriction. This is determined by the route change flag, which must be cleared whenever a route has been included in a round of advertisements.

If a periodic update should occur before the delay interval expires, the triggered update must be canceled.

9.3.3 Expiration and Deletion Timers

The expiration timer marks a route as unreachable if the route has not been updated in 180 seconds, which is six periodic update intervals. This allows a few updates to be lost by the network before the route is considered bad. The chosen value is a compromise between the desire for rapid detection of failures and the desire to avoid spurious failure indications (which would generate triggered updates). Whenever a route is updated, it resets this timer. The route is marked invalid (usually by setting the metric to 16) rather than being deleted because RIP needs to be able to advertise the route with its new metric. Note that expiration constitutes a change to the route, which must be flagged and which will initiate a triggered update.

When a route becomes invalid, because it has either expired or been set to invalid by its next hop, a garbage collection timer is set for 120 seconds, which is four periodic update intervals. During this time, the invalid route is included in the periodic updates to indicate to the neighboring routers that the route is, in fact, invalid. If this were not done, those routers would have to depend on timeouts (of 180 seconds) to discover that the route was invalid. When this timer expires, the route is deleted from the routing table. If this route should be reestablished prior to deletion, the new next hop and/or metric is inserted and the garbage collection timer is canceled.

9.4 Input Processing

A router can receive one of two message types: a request for routing table information and a response containing routing table information. In addition, there are currently two versions of RIP deployed in the Internet. As each step in the message-handling process is discussed, features unique to each version are called out.

9.4.1 Request Messages

There are two forms of request message: requests for information about a select set of routes and requests for the entire routing table.

Requests for a set of routes are generally created by network administrator applications to debug routing problems in the network. They are sent (usually unicast) to the UDP routing port (520), and contain an ephemeral source port, to which the router directs its (unicast) response. The request contains a set of up to 25 RIP entries (24 if authentication is in use) that contain only address family IDs and destination addresses (all other fields must be zero). See Section 9.5.2 Responses to Requests for the construction of the response message.

Requests for the entire routing table are generally made by routers that have just come up and are trying to fill in their routing tables. They could also wait (a kind of slow start) for 30 seconds (one periodic advertisement interval) to gather the routes via periodic updates. These requests are usually sent to the IP broadcast address. Version 2 requests are sent to the RIP multicast address, which only RIP-2 routers will receive. In either case, they are sent to the routing port. The source port is also the routing port (as opposed to an ephemeral port); otherwise, the routing process would not receive the response(s). A request for the entire routing table must contain only a single RIP entry. That entry must contain a metric of 16 and *all* other fields must be zero. In response to this request, a router will instruct its output process to generate a routing table update. It should be identical to the periodic updates (including split horizon and administrative restrictions for the interface over which the response will be generated), except that the response is sent as a unicast to the originator of the request.

For both types of request, the version of the response should match the version of the request. If, for administrative reasons, both versions are accepted but only one version is advertised, then a request using the nonadvertised version must be ignored.

If version 2 with authentication is in use, the request must also be authenticated. An unauthenticated request must be ignored. If authentication is in use and both versions are allowed (a peculiar combination), then version 1 requests should receive responses.

9.4.2 Response Messages

Response messages are generated for three reasons:

1. A response to a request
2. A periodic (unsolicited) advertisement
3. A triggered update

However, the algorithm for handling responses is the same for each case.

The first step in response processing is validation. Because response messages might update the contents of the routing table, they must be checked very carefully. The following message-validation tests must be performed prior to processing the individual entries. If any test fails, the entire message must be discarded. No indication of failure is reported to the originator of the message, but some form of logging and/or statistic is desirable.

- The response must be *from* the RIP port (obviously it went *to* the RIP port or it wouldn't be here).

- The IP address of the originator of the response must be a valid neighbor. That is, it must either be the remote address on a point-to-point link, or an address on a directly connected broadcast or LAN.

- If the response is from one of the router's own interfaces (e.g., the subnet received a copy of its own broadcast/multicast), it should be discarded.

- Most implementations also check to ensure that the response is of correct length. After removing the headers, the length must be an integral multiple of the size of the individual entries (and no more than 25 of them).

- The version must be acceptable to the current configuration. A version 0 response must be discarded. If any other administrative restrictions are in place (e.g., a router list), they must also be satisfied.

- For versions 1 and 2, the "must be zero" field in the header must be zero. The field should be ignored for versions 3 and later.

Once the message has passed the basic validation tests, each route entry must be processed. Again, this processing begins with validation testing. If any test is failed, the entry is ignored and processing proceeds with the next entry. Some form of logging and/or statistic is desirable.

- The destination address must be a valid, IPv4, unicast address (or the default address, 0.0.0.0). It must not be an address on net 0 or net 127 (loopback). Invalid addresses are often referred to as **Martians**.

- The metric must be a value from 1 to 16.

- If the response is version 1, the "must be zero" fields in the entry must be zero.

- If the response is version 2, the next hop, if present, must be a valid, IPv4, unicast address. It must not be net 0 or net 127.

Depending on the implementation, the next hop may have to be a neighbor (as previously defined); however, there are strategies that do not require this.

If the response is version 2, and the first entry is an authentication, and authentication is in use, authenticate the response (see Section 9.6 Authentication). If authentication is not in use, discard the entire response. If authentication fails, discard the entire response. In either case, some form of logging is desirable.

Once the entry has been validated, add to the metric the cost of the interface over which the response arrived. If the new metric is greater than 16, use 16 (there's nothing beyond infinity).

If the destination address exactly matches an entry in the routing table, then this is an update; otherwise, it is a new entry. If the response is version 2, the address and subnet mask must *both* be compared. If this is a new route and its metric is 16, do not add it to the table (it would only be deleted in 120 seconds anyway).

Perform the following steps to add a route to the routing table:

- Set the destination address to the destination address in the update. If the response is version 2, the subnet mask must be saved; otherwise, the assumed subnet mask must be saved.
- Set the metric to the calculated metric.
- Set the next hop address to the address of the router that generated the response. If the response is version 2 and a next hop has been specified, save that address instead.
- If the response is version 2, save the route tag.
- Set the expiration timer for the route.
- Set the route change flag.

Perform the following steps to update a route that already exists in the routing table:

- If the response is from the route's next hop (or, for version 2, the next hop addresses match), reset the expiration timer and compare the metrics. If the metrics are the same, proceed to the next response entry. If the metrics are different, update the metric in the routing table and set the route change flag. If the new metric is 16, clear the expiration timer and set the garbage collection timer. If the old metric was 16, clear the garbage collection timer and set the expiration timer.

- If the response is from a different next hop and the new metric is lower, reset the expiration timer, update the next hop and metric with the new values, and set the route change flag. If the new metric is higher, proceed to the next response entry (do *not* reset the expiration timer). A commonly implemented heuristic is to update the route if the metrics are the same *and* the existing route's age is at least halfway to its expiration time. This practice reduces convergence time.

Once all response entries have been processed, if changes have been made to the routing table, a triggered update should be scheduled.

9.5 Output Processing

There are four reasons to generate output:

1. A request for a full routing table
2. A response to a request
3. Periodic (unsolicited) routing advertisements
4. Triggered updates

Note that the first is a request message and the others are response messages.

9.5.1 Initial Request

The initial request message is generated when RIP first starts up. It is used to gather routing information from the router's neighbors as quickly as possible. The alternative is to wait until all of the neighbors have had a chance to send their periodic updates (30 seconds). Some router implementations send this request (or allow it to be configured), others do not.

To generate the request, a RIP message is created (see Section 9.1 Message Format). The **command** is set to **request**, and **version** is set to the configured value. If authentication is in use, the first RIP entry contains the authentication information (see Section 9.6 Authentication).

Aside from any authentication entry, the message must contain only a single RIP entry. All of the fields in the entry must be zero, except for the **metric**, which must be 16. The message is sent to the router port, from the router port. On links that support broadcasting (e.g., Ethernet), version 1 requests are sent to the IP broadcast address and version 2 requests are sent to the RIP multicast address. On point-to-point links, the requests are sent (unicast) to the remote end of the link (although some implementations broadcast/multicast, which is permissible).

9.5.2 Responses to Requests

A request can be for a portion of the routing table or for the entire routing table. If it is for a partial routing table, the request contains a set of up to 25 RIP entries (24 if authentication is in use) that contain only address family IDs and destination addresses (all other fields must be zero). For each entry, the queried router looks up the address in its routing table and fills in the metric. If there is no explicit route (i.e., the default route is not considered), the metric 16 (infinity) is inserted. Note that no split horizon is applied (whether administrative restrictions are applied is implementation-specific). For version 2 requests, the subnet mask, route tag, and (at the implementer's and administrator's discretion) next hop are also filled in. Once all of the routes have been handled, **command** is changed from **request** to **response**, and the message is sent to the originator of the request. Note that the version is unchanged.

If the request is for the entire routing table, the same code that generates periodic responses may be used to generate the response. The code must base its split horizon and administrative restriction decisions on the interface over which the response will be sent. The response should be sent directly (unicast) to the querying node. It should *not* cause a reset of the route change flags.

9.5.3 Periodic Responses

To generate a periodic response, a RIP message (see Section 9.1 Message Format) is created. The **command** is set to **response**, and **version** is set to the configured value. If authentication is in use, the first RIP entry contains the authentication information (see Section 9.6 Authentication).

Next, the entire routing table must be examined to determine which entries should be included in the update. If a route is eliminated due to split horizon (see Section 8.2.3 Split Horizon) or administrative restriction, skip it. Any local loopback routes should be omitted. Routes with metrics of 16 must be included. To add a routing entry to the update:

- If the update is version 1, zero the "must be zero" fields.
- Set **destination address** and **metric**. If the route is a poison reverse entry, the metric is set to 16.
- If the update is for version 2, set **subnet mask** and **route tag**. Set **next hop** if necessary/configured (for an example, see the **rip_next_hop** parameter in Section 6.1.3). Note that a router should *not* poison routes for another next hop.

Response messages can hold, at most, 25 RIP entries (24 if authentication is in use). Once a message is full, it is transmitted and another is constructed. It is not typically necessary to insert a delay between transmissions; the time it takes to construct a message is sufficient. The response is sent to the router port, from the router port. On links that support broadcasting, version 1 responses are sent to the IP broadcast address and version 2 responses are sent to the RIP multicast address. On point-to-point links, the responses are sent to the remote end of the link.

This algorithm is executed for each interface. Because of split horizon, it is not possible to simply send the same response message on every interface.

Once all interfaces have been handled, the route change flags should be reset.

9.5.4 Triggered Updates

A triggered update is constructed in the same way, and with the same rules, as a periodic response. However, there are some additional considerations that reduce network load while still expediting convergence.

When a route is changed, it does not cause a triggered update to be *sent*; it causes a triggered update to be *scheduled*. The difference is the time interval between the change and the sending of the update (usually a random interval between 1 and 5 seconds). This interval has two effects: It allows multiple routes to change, and be included, in a single update; and it limits the number of triggered updates that can be generated per minute. If a periodic update should be generated prior to a scheduled triggered update, the triggered update should be canceled (because the new information has already been advertised).

A triggered update should include only those routes that have changed since the last update (triggered or periodic). That is, routes whose route change flag is set. This allows rapid dissemination of new information without the overhead of information that is already known to the neighbors. If, after split horizon and administrative restriction processing, a route appears unchanged on an interface, it may be omitted from the update. If no routes need to be advertised on an interface, no update is sent. That is, do not send an empty update (it's not harmful, just wasteful). If a triggered update is large enough to require multiple response messages, no delay needs to be inserted between them.

Once all interfaces have been handled, the route change flags should be reset. It is important *not* to reset the flags after the first interface's update because subsequent interfaces will never detect the changes.

One additional consideration is the interlocking of input and output processing. If these processes are permitted to operate in parallel (an implementation-dependent detail), some form of lock must be established to prevent changes to the route change flags while triggered updates are being generated. Otherwise, different information might be sent to different interfaces. Although this situation would be corrected eventually, it is preferable to prevent it.

Finally, the sending of a triggered update should not affect the timing of the periodic updates. For example, if 15 seconds has elapsed since the last periodic update when a triggered update is sent, the next periodic update must occur in 15 seconds (not 30 seconds).

9.5.5 The Broadcast Address

There are two forms of broadcast address that a router might use. The first form is the limited broadcast. It is defined as 255.255.255.255. A router must never forward a packet sent to this address (with a very special exception made for BOOTP/DHCP). The other form is the directed subnet broadcast. It is defined as net.subnet.255 (e.g., the directed subnet broadcast address for 132.245.33.0/24 would be 132.245.33.255). Under certain conditions, these packets may be forwarded to a limited area [Mogul 1984a, b]. The broadcast address used is implementation-specific.

9.6 Authentication

Authentication is new to RIP-2. It was added because the IETF requires all protocols to include security. The basic security defined in the RIP-2 specification is sufficient for networks that are physically secure (i.e., networks that cannot be tapped from the outside). Security against more aggressive attack has been defined in Baker and Atkinson [1987].

Since there is no notion of a connection between RIP-2 routers, and RIP messages are independent of previous and succeeding messages, authentication is a per-message function. That is, each message must be authenticated in a self-contained way. The problem is that RIP-2 messages have only a single, 2-octet field available. Obviously, this is insufficient to do any real authentication. Therefore, the first entry of an authenticated RIP-2 message contains the authentication information (providing 20 octets).

If the first (and only the first) RIP entry has an **address family ID** of 0xFFFF, then this is an authenticated message and the remainder of the entry contains the additional authentication information. An authentication entry has the format shown in Figure 9.4.

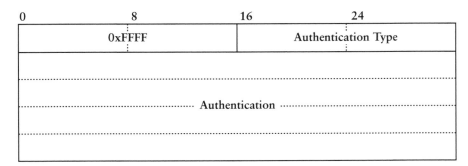

Figure 9.4. RIP-2 authentication entry format

Authentication type is a 2-octet field that specifies the type of authentication in use. The types supported by RIP-2 are

- 2—clear-text password. This is the only mechanism defined in the RIP-2 specification.
- 3—keyed MD-5. This is defined in Baker and Atkinson 1987.

Note that there is no type for "none." If no authentication is in use, this entry is not included in the message.

Authentication is a 16-octet field that contains the authentication information. For clear-text password authentication, this contains the password (left-justified and padded to the right with nulls, if necessary). Note that there is nothing restricting the contents of the password (e.g., it doesn't have to be ASCII).

9.6.1 Keyed MD-5

If keyed MD-5 is in use, the authentication field contains some of the values required for generating and locating, within the packet, the cryptographic checksum. Since keyed MD-5 requires more than 16 octets for operation, a trailer is added to the end of the RIP-2 message to form the authenticated packet. The format of an authenticated RIP-2 packet is shown in Figure 9.5.

The gray fields represent variable length fields. The **command** and **version** fields have the standard definitions. "0xFFFF" indicates an authentication entry, and "3" indicates keyed MD-5 authentication.

RIP-2 packet length contains the length, in octets, of the RIP-2 message from **command** to the end of the last RIP entry, inclusive. This includes the length of the authentication entry, as it is embedded in the message, but not the length of the trailer. This value is used to find the starting point of the authentication information appended to the message.

Key ID contains the key identifier used to create the authentication trailer for the packet.

Auth data length contains the length, in octets, of the **authentication data** field.

Sequence number is a 32-bit field that contains the sequence number of the packet. The values in this field must only increase from packet to packet. This is necessary to prevent "play-back" attacks.

0	8	16	24
Command	Version	Must be zero	
0xFFFF		3	
RIP-2 Packet Length		Key ID	Auth Data Length
Sequence Number			
Must be zero			
Must be zero			
1–24 RIP Entries			
0xFFFF		0x01	
Authentication Data			

Figure 9.5. Authenticated RIP-2 packet

Authentication data contains the output of the MD-5 algorithm, which is always 16 octets in length. The field is of variable length to support other authentication algorithms in the future.

To generate an authenticated packet, the RIP-2 message is constructed as usual (see Section 9.5 Output Processing). The first RIP entry of the message is an authentication entry that specifies keyed MD-5 authentication (authentication type 3). The fields shown in authentication entry in Figure 9.5 are filled in appropriately.

The sequence number is arbitrary, except that it must be nondecreasing. Two suggestions are the time (real-time; not time since boot) or a monotonically increasing counter. The problem with a counter is that it will reset across boots. This problem can be reduced, but not eliminated, by initializing the counter with the time of day.

On reception, if the calculated message digest does not match the received message digest, the entire message is discarded. If a valid message has been heard from the neighbor recently enough that there are valid routes through it, and the sequence number of the message is less than the sequence number in the last valid message, the entire message is discarded (it is either old or a replay). If a message is discarded, no notification is sent to the originator of the message, but some form of logging and/or statistic is desirable.

Many of the details of the MD5 algorithm and the key distribution mechanism are not discussed in this book, because they are outside the scope of the RIP protocol itself. Interested readers are referred to the references.

9.6.2 Authentication Matrix

The matrix in Table 9.2 describes how to handle authenticated messages. The matrix assumes that the version 2 (V2) routers are willing to accept version 1 (V1) messages, and that they are running in compatibility mode. If the V2 routers are sending RIP-2 only (which is recommended), then some of the cases will not occur. Note that V1 routers accept authenticated packets, but ignore the authentication entry as being from an unsupported address family. Of course, when the authentication methods do match, authentication must succeed for the message to be accepted. This matrix applies to requests and responses.

Table 9.2. Authentication Matrix

msg router	V1 n/a	V2 none	V2 pswd	V2 MD-5
V1	n/a	accept	accept	accept	accept
	none	accept	accept	reject	reject
	pswd	reject	reject	accept	reject
	MD-5	reject	reject	reject	accept

10

RIP MIB

The IETF requires that all protocols support a Management Information Base (MIB) for Simple Network Management Protocol (SNMP) management. The MIB for RIP is defined in Malkin and Baker [1994].

Only the objects currently in use are described; obsolete and deprecated objects are not included.

10.1 Global Counters

The global counters are cumulative across inferfaces. They do not need to be preserved across system reboot.

- rip2GlobalRouteChanges—This object counts the number of changes made to the IP routing database. It does not include refreshes of a route's age.

- rip2GlobalQueries—This object counts the number of responses to requests from other systems.

10.2 Interface Statistics Table

The objects in an interface statistics table of a MIB are maintained on a per-interface basis. The table is indexed by the interface number.

- rip2IfStatAddress—This object is the IP address of the interface. The MIB specifies that unnumbered addresses are encoded as 0.0.0.N, where N is the ifIndex for the interface. However, RIP does not formally support unnumbered interfaces.

- rip2IfStatRcvBadRoutes—This object counts the number of routes, in valid RIP entries, that were ignored for any reason (e.g., unknown address family, invalid metric).

- rip2IfStatSentUpdates—This object counts the number of triggered updates actually sent on this interface. It explicitly does *not* include periodic updates, even if they contain new information.

- rip2IfStatStatus—This object indicates the status of the interface. Writing "invalid" to this object will delete the interface.

10.3 Interface Configuration Table

The objects in an interface configuration table of a MIB are maintained on a per-interface basis. The table is indexed by the interface number.

- rip2IfConfAddress—This object is the IP address of the interface. The MIB specifies that unnumbered addresses are encoded as 0.0.0.N, where N is the ifIndex for the interface. However, RIP does not formally support unnumbered interfaces.

- rip2IfConfAuthType—This object is the type of authentication in use on the interface. There are three defined values for this object: noAuthentication (1), simplePassword (2), and md5 (3). The default is noAuthentication.

- rip2IfConfAuthKey—This object is the password/key to be used whenever the authentication type is other than noAuthentication. The maximum length of the field is 16 octets. If the value is less than 16 octets, it is left-justified and padded to the right with nulls. Reading this object always returns a zero-length string.

- rip2IfConfSend—This object is the version of RIP that should be sent on this interface. There are six defined values for this object: doNotSend (1), ripVersion1 (2), rip1Compatible (3), ripVersion2 (4), ripV1Demand (5), and ripV2Demand (6). The latter two values are defined to support RIP for Demand Circuit Routes [Meyer and Sherry 1997]. The default is ripVersion2.

- rip2IfConfReceive—This object is the version(s) of RIP that should be accepted in this interface. There are four defined values for this object: rip1 (1), rip2 (2), rip1OrRip2 (3), and doNotReceive (4). Note that rip2 and rip1OrRip2 imply reception of RIP multicast packets.

- rip2IfConfDefaultMetric—This object is the metric that should be used for the default route entry in RIP updates generated for this interface. A value of zero indicates that no default route should be generated, in which case a learned default route may be propagated.

- rip2IfConfStatus—This object indicates the status of the interface. Writing "invalid" to this object will delete the interface.

- rip2IfConfSrcAddress—This object is the IP address RIP will use as a source address for messages sent on this interface. For numbered interfaces, this value must match rip2IfConfAddress. For unnumbered interfaces, it must be the rip2IfConfAddress for some interface on the system. Note that RIP does not formally support unnumbered interfaces.

10.4 Peer Table

The objects in a peer table of a MIB are maintained on a per-peer basis. An active peer is any neighbor from which a valid RIP update has been received in the last 180 seconds. The table is indexed by peer IP address.

- rip2PeerAddress—This object is the IP address that the peer is using as its IP address on the interface that the peers share.

- rip2PeerLastUpdate—This object is the value of sysUpTime when the most recent valid RIP update was received from this peer.

- rip2Peer Version—This object is the version number of the most recent valid RIP update received from this peer.

- rip2PeerRcvBadPackets—This object counts the number of RIP response packets from this peer that have been discarded as invalid.

- rip2PeerRcvBadRoutes—This object counts the number of routes received from this peer that were ignored for invalid entry format.

Many implementations do not implement the peer table because they do not keep track of neighbors for any operational reason. Remember that RIP is stateless and does not need to "know" about neighbors. The peer table is purely statistical.

Glossary

Most of the entries in this glossary are taken from RFC 1983 (FYI 18).

Acceptable Use Policy (AUP) An agreement (usually between an ISP and its subscribers) that defines how the network may be used and what usage, if any, is prohibited.

asymmetric routing A situation in which multiple paths exist between two nodes, and packets from node A to node B take a different path than packets take from node B to node A. There is nothing inherently "bad" about this situation.

backbone The "central" subnet of a network to which other stub networks are attached (with routers). A backbone is a transit network.

big-endian A format for storage or transmission of binary data in which the most significant bit (or byte) comes first. The term comes from *Gulliver's Travels* by Jonathan Swift. The Lilliputians, being very small, had correspondingly small political problems. The Big-Endian and Little-Endian parties debated whether soft-boiled eggs should be opened at the big end or the little end.

black hole A route that leads to a failed or nonexistent node or network; so called because packets sent to that destination are never heard from again (i.e., no error message is generated that indicates to the source that the packet has been lost).

border router A router that resides on the edge of two or more routing domains and is responsible for forwarding packets between them.

bridge A layer 2 device that connects multiple network segments. Network segments that have been "bridged" appear as a single entity to the network layer.

broadcast address A special IP address that is accepted by all IP nodes. There are three types of IP broadcast address. A general (limited) broadcast is only transmitted on a single subnet (i.e., it is never forwarded). Its value is 255.255.255.255. A network-directed broadcast may, under certain circumstances, be forwarded to all subnets within a specific network. Its value is network.-1 (e.g., 132.245.255.255/16). A subnet-directed broadcast may, under certain circumstances, be forwarded to a specific subnet. Its value is network.subnet.-1 (e.g., 132.245.8.255/24).

byte order The order in which the bytes of a word occur. In big-endian, the most significant byte is the leftmost byte of the word. In little-endian (also called byte-swapped), the most significant byte is the rightmost byte of the word.

Classless InterDomain Routing (CIDR) An IETF proposal to make more of the 32-bit IP address space available. It makes the address/mask pair a 64-bit entity, which removes the need to determine the network mask using the top three bits of the address. This allows for a single-bit granularity in address assignment, rather than 8-bit granularity.

convergence time The elapsed time between the detection of a change in a network's topology and the updating of all routers responsible for knowing that topology.

cost An indication of how much of something it takes to reach a given destination. *Cost* might refer to the number of hops, the speed or reliability of a link, the transit time, or any combination of these or other factors.

counting to infinity A condition that occurs when routers advertise an invalid route to each other. Each router increments the metric until it reaches infinity (16 in RIP), at which point the route is discarded.

Customer Premise Equipment (CPE) The device(s) within a subscriber's network that connect the subscriber to a service provider. The router that connects a site to its ISP is an example of a CPE.

datagram A self-contained, independent entity of data that is carrying sufficient information to be routed from the source node to the destination node without reliance on earlier exchanges between this source and destination. A datagram may also be referred to as a layer 3 packet. It contains a layer 3 (IP) header and layer 4 data.

default route This route, identified by the IP address 0.0.0.0/0, is the route a router chooses when it does not have a better route to use. Note that 0.0.0.0/x is an invalid address for all values of x except 0.

diameter The shortest distance between the two most distant nodes in a network.

directly connected network A network segment that is attached to an interface on the node. Such a network is said to be "directly reachable."

distance-vector algorithm A routing algorithm that operates by locally distributing global information. That is, each router sends to its neighbors (local distribution) its entire routing table (global information). RIP is an example of a distance-vector routing algorithm.

domain name A name of the form *subdomain.tld,* where "subdomain" is a unique name assigned to a network under the top-level domain, "tld" (e.g. com, edu, us). These names are converted by the Domain Name System (DNS) into IP addresses.

dynamic adaptive routing The process of automatically rerouting packets based on a sensing and analysis of current, actual network conditions.

expiration time The amount of time a router considers a route valid after it has received an update for that route.

flooding A process by which information is distributed to a set of nodes on a network. It usually involves sending the same information over every interface (except the one over which the information was received).

forwarding The process of accepting a packet on one interface and trans-mitting it over another interface. The choice of the outgoing interface is determined by routing.

frame A layer 2 unit of information that consists of a layer 2 header, layer 3 data, and possibly a layer 2 trailer.

garbage collection time The amount of time a router keeps an expired route in its routing table before deleting it. During this time, a route is advertised as unreachable and is not used to route packets.

gateway An obsolete name for a router. However, a "layer 3 gateway" is a router; a "layer 2 gateway" is a bridge. There are also application gateways that perform application-specific functions.

hierarchical topology A network topology in which multiple stub networks are attached (with routers) to a backbone network.

host A node on a network that generates and accepts packets for itself. It does not forward traffic for other nodes (as does a router).

host byte order The order in which the bytes of a word are represented on the host. For example, Intel microprocessors use little-endian (also called byte-swapped) order. Almost everyone else uses big-endian order.

host route A route whose destination address is a host address (i.e., an address whose host mask is 32 1-bits).

Internet Control Message Protocol (ICMP) A required extension to the Internet Protocol, ICMP allows for the generation of error messages, test packets, and informational messages related to the operation of IP. The original message types are defined in Postel [1981]. Later message types are defined in their own RFCs.

Internet Registry The Internet authority that assigns IP addresses to organizations for use in their networks. Addresses that have been so assigned are referred to as "globally unique."

Internet service provider (ISP) An organization that provides access to the Internet for other organizations or individual users.

intrinsic network mask When the Internet Protocol was first created, there were three classes of IP address—A, B, and C—and each had a network mask associated with it. The masks are described in Table 9.1.

IPv4 The shorthand notation for Internet Protocol (IP) version 4, which is the network layer protocol on which the Internet has been built.

IPv6 The shorthand notation for Internet Protocol version 6.

LAN (Local Area Network) A data network intended to serve an area of only a few square kilometers or smaller. Given this restriction, optimizations to the signaling protocols permit very high data rates.

learned route A route that is received from another router via a routing protocol; also called a dynamic route.

link A physical network segment that connects multiple nodes. An Ethernet segment is a link, as is a serial line.

link failure The failure of a link in a network. The failure of a node's interface to a link may also be interpreted as a link failure by that node.

link state A routing algorithm that operates by globally distributing local information. That is, each router sends to all other routers (global distribution) the state of its links (local information). With this information, a router can create a map of the entire network. OSPF is an example of a link state routing algorithm.

little-endian A format for storage or transmission of binary data in which the least significant bit (or byte) comes first.

longest match An IP address-matching algorithm in which the address with the longest subnet mask (i.e., the mask with the most 1-bits) is preferred over the same address with shorter masks. For example, 132.245.66.1/32 is preferred over 132.245.66.0/24, which is preferred over 132.245.0.0/16, and so on.

Martian An invalid IP source address or route destination address. Usually, net 0, net 127, and multicast/broadcast addresses are considered Martians, even though they may be valid in other contexts.

multicast address An IP address in the range from 224.0.0.1 to 239.255.255.254. These addresses are assigned to specific protocols and are sent to multiple nodes. Those nodes may be configured to receive any number of them. 224.0.0.1 is the "all IP nodes" address; 224.0.0.2 is the "all IP routers" address; 224.0.0.9 is the RIP-2 multicast address.

neighbor Any node that can be reached without passing through a router. For example, all of the nodes on a LAN are neighbors, as are the end points of a serial link.

network byte order The order in which the bytes of a word are transmitted on a network. This is almost always big-endian order.

network mask The mask that, when applied to an IP address, yields the network address portion of the IP address. The portion of the IP address that is masked off is the host (or subnet and host) portion.

network route A route whose destination address is a network address (i.e., an address whose mask is the intrinsic mask associated with the address).

next hop The next node, from the current node's point of view, to which a packet must be sent in order to reach that packet's destination. For the last router in the route, the next hop is the destination itself.

packet A discrete unit of information that travels through a network. Specifically, it refers to application data. Generically, it may be used to refer to a frame or datagram.

periodic update An unsolicited routing advertisement (update) that is sent at regular intervals. RIP updates are sent approximately every 30 seconds.

Point of Presence (POP) A site within a network where there exists equipment that connects subscribers to that network. A telephone company's central office is an example of a POP.

poison reverse An algorithm that states that routes learned on a given interface should be re-advertised over that interface with a metric of infinity.

Remote Access Server (RAS) A network device that terminates multiple dial-up links and forwards packets between those links and the network to which the RAS is connected.

Request for Comments (RFC) The document series, begun in 1969, that describes the Internet suite of protocols and related experiments. Very few RFCs actually describe Internet standards, but all Internet standards are written up as RFCs. The FYIs (informational documents), STDs (standards specifications), and BCPs (best current practice descriptions) are subseries of RFCs.

route The path a packet takes from its source to its destination. As an entry within a router's routing table, a route usually consists of a destination address, next hop, metric, age, and control information.

route change flag An indication to the routing process that the route has been recently added, modified, or expired.

router A layer 3 device that forwards packets between networks. The routing decision is based on network layer information in the packets and routing tables constructed by the router (often using routing protocols).

routing The process of determining the best path for a packet to take as it travels from its source to its destination.

routing domain A group of routers that use the same routing protocol to exchange routing information.

split horizon An algorithm that states that routes learned on a given interface should not be re-advertised over that interface.

star topology A network topology in which multiple subnets are connected to a single hub (usually a router). It has the advantage of creating only a single hop between networks, but has the disadvantage of creating a single point of failure.

static route A route configured by a network administrator. It does not reflect changes to a network's topology (as does a learned route).

stub network A network that carries packets only to and from the nodes attached to it. It does not carry packets for nodes on other networks (as does a transit network).

subnet An independently addressable portion of a network. See Section 2.3 Subnets and Supernets.

subnet mask The mask that, when applied to an IP address, yields the subnet address portion of that IP address. The portion of the IP address that is masked is the host portion.

subnet route A route whose destination address is a subnet address (i.e., an address with a mask that is longer than the intrinsic network mask, yet not a host mask).

supernet A collection of independently addressable networks that have been aggregated under a single IP address. See Section 2.3 Subnets and Supernets.

system failure The failure of a node on a network that affects the operation of that network (e.g., a router failure).

tick A measurement of time, approximately 1/18 of a second.

topology The physical structure of a network, including the nodes (hosts and routers) and links that connect them.

transit network A network that carries packets for nodes attached to it, and for nodes on other networks. A backbone network is a transit network.

tree-structured topology A network topology in which there is only a single path between any two subnets, and the diameter of the network grows with the addition of each new router.

triggered update An unsolicited routing advertisement (update) that is generated in response to a change to a router's routing table.

variable length subnetting The use of different length subnet masks on network segments within a network. The purpose is to maximize the use of the IP address pool by defining subnets with host address ranges no larger than necessary to accommodate the numbers of hosts on those subnets.

WAN (Wide Area Network) A network, usually constructed with serial lines, that covers a large geographic area.

References

Baker, F, and R. Atkinson, "RIP-2 MD5 Authentication," RFC 2082, January 1997.

Bellman, R. E., *Dynamic Programming,* Princeton, NJ: Princeton University Press, 1987.

Bertsekas, D. P., and R. G. Gallaher, *Data Networks,* Englewood Cliffs, NJ: Prentice-Hall, 1957.

Boggs, D. R., et al., "PUP: An Internetwork Architecture," *IEEE Transactions on Communications,* April 1980.

Case, J.D., M. Fedor, M. L. Schoffstall, and C. Davin, "Simple Network Management Protocol (SNMP)," RFC 1157 (STD 15), May 1990.

Deering, S., and R. Hinden, "Internet Protocol Version 6 (IPv6) Specification," RFC 2460, December 1998.

Floyd, S., and V. Jacobson, "The Synchronization of Periodic Routing Messages," ACM Sigcom Symposium, September 1993.

Ford, L. R., Jr., and D. R. Fulkerson, *Flows in Networks,* Princeton, NJ: Princeton University Press, 1962.

Hedrick, C., "Routing Information Protocol," RFC 1058 (STD 34), June 1988.

Malkin, G. S., "RIP Version 2: Carrying Additional Information," RFC 2453 (STD 56), November 1998.

Malkin, G. S., and F. Baker, "RIP Version 2 MIB Extension," RFC 1724, November 1994.

Malkin, G. S., and R. Minnear, "RIPng for IPv6," RFC 2080, January 1997.

Meyer, G., and S. Sherry, "Triggered Extensions to Support Demand Circuits," RFC 2091, January 1997.

Mogul, J. C., "Broadcasting Internet Datagrams," RFC 0919 (STD 5), October 1984a.

———, "Broadcasting Internet Datagrams in the Presence of Subnets," RFC 0922 (STD 5), October 1984b.

Moy, J., "OSPF Version 2," RFC 2328 (STD 54), April 1998.

Perlman, R., *Interconnections: Bridges and Routers,* Reading, MA: Addison-Wesley Publishing Company, 1992.

Postel, J., "Internet Control Message Protocol," RFC 0792, September 1981.

Sedgewick, R., *Algorithms,* Reading, MA: Addison-Wesley Publishing Company, 1983.

Xerox Corporation, "Internet Transport Protocols," Xerox System Integration Standard XSIS 028112, December 1981.

Index